THE NATURE OF THINGS
De rerum natura

Author: Lucretius
4/22/2013

THE NATURE OF THINGS

Table of Contents

Introduction by Marciano Guerrero iv
About *De rerum natura* iv
BOOK ONE — MATTER AND SPACE 1
   1 — Invocation to Venus 1
   2 — Dedication to Memmius 2
   3 — On superstition 2
   4 — The nature of the universe 4
   5 — First principle of nature 5
   6 — The second principle of nature 7
   7 — About Atoms 8
   8 — Vacuity 10
   9 — Bodies and vacant space 13
   10 — Property, accidents, and time 14
   11 — Atoms and compounds 15
   12 — Heraclitus' theory 19
   13 — My poetry and my reward 27
   14 — The boundless universe 28
BOOK TWO — MOVEMENTS AND SHAPES OF ATOMS 32
   15 — Body and mind 32
   16 — New business: Birth, motion, and decay 34
   17 — The motion of the atoms 37
   18 — About determinism and free will 39
   19 — The supply of matter in the universe 41
   20 — About the shapes and forms of matter 42
   21 — About colors 53
   22 — About other sensory qualities 56

THE NATURE OF THINGS

23 — Of things sentient and insentient 57
24 — Other earths, other races of men 62
BOOK THREE — LIFE AND MIND 66
25 — A prayer 66
26 — Mind 67
27 — Spirit 70
28 — Mind and its matter 71
29 — A 'fourth element' rules the spirit 73
30 — Minds and spirits: no birth no death 78

Introduction by Marciano Guerrero

Titus Lucretius Carus (c. 98-55 B.C.) was a Roman poet who wrote *De rerum natura* (On the Nature of Things). *De rerum natura* is an epic poem which explains life and the world in incipient atomic principles. In his poem Lucretius adheres to principles as set by philosopher Epicurus.

St. Jerome says that Lucretius committed suicide at the age of 44; furthermore, that Lucretius wrote the work between bouts of madness. None of this has been confirmed. What is clear is his allegiance to Gaius Memmius —an aristocrat married to Fausta, the daughter of the dictator Sulla— to whom he dedicates the work, mentioning him repeatedly throughout the six books.

About *De rerum natura*

What is astounding about this epic poem is that it was written more than 2,000 years ago, when the Roman universe was still accounted for by heroes, demigods, and gods—both native and imported.

From the very beginning one feels the athletic language of a poet determined to explain things and creatures in simple language. Although he frequently complains about the "poverty" of Latin to explain the concepts he had in mind, he never gives up in his efforts; at worst his verses reveal a clear-headed poet.

The task he set for himself —to anyone else— would have been too daunting to tackle, yet patiently he attempts to demolish old theories and traditions that had for too long overcome good sense. He deeply believed that matter consisted of minute building blocks he called atoms that their conjunction would spawn things and creatures—including sentient beings. Yet, one tradition —the Aristotelian— was difficult for Lucretius to overthrow, given the tremendous authority that Aristotle's teaching had garnered over the years. As time and experience has proven, Lucretius eventually won the battle.

De rerum natura miraculously has survived wars, lootings, burnings, and other calamities; and worst of all: censoring. Harvard Shakespearean scholar Stephen Greenblatt, in his book *The Swerve*, shows how Lucretius helped to shape the Renaissance, the Scientific Revolution, and how Lucretius' poem was so unwelcome by the Catholic Church; but more importantly, how "at the core of the poem lay key principles of a modern understanding of the world."

From Machiavelli, Montaigne, Thomas More, to Thomas Jefferson—Lucretius's poem continues to exert great influence even today as the 'creationism-evolution' unfolds.

My translation of books I, II, and III is rendered in prose and in American English for the benefit of impatient readers who find it tedious to read a long poem from beginning to end. The book is a great investment that will pay great intellectual dividends in perpetuity.

BOOK ONE — MATTER AND SPACE

1 — Invocation to Venus

Life-giving Venus, mother of Aeneas and his race, delight of men and gods, who makes nature teem with life, under the wheeling constellations of the sky; and the sea that buoys up our ships and the earth that grows our food as well.

Through you all living beings are conceived and come forth to look upon the sunlight. Before you the winds flee, and at your wish the clouds disperse from the sky. For you the creative earth sprouts up sweet flowers, the ocean levels laugh, and the sky calms and glows with gentle radiance.

When the first spring day shows itself, when in all its force the fertilizing breath of Zephyr[1] is unleashed, then great goddess, the birds of air give the first hint of your entry. Yours is the power that pierces them to the heart. Next the wild beasts and farm animals alike run wild, frisking through the lush pastures, swimming the swift-flowing streams. Enchanted by your charm, they follow your lead with intense desire. Instilling your alluring love, throughout seas and uplands, rushing torrents, verdant meadows and the leafy nests of the birds, into the breasts of one and all you fill them with deep longing to multiply their several breeds.

You alone are the guiding power of the universe and without you nothing comes into the shining sunlit world to grow with joy and love; so, yours is the partnership I seek in striving to write these lines *On the Nature of the Universe* for my noble Memmius.[2] For him, great goddess, you have willed unmatched excellence in every field and everlasting fame. For his honor, therefore, endow my verse with everlasting value.

Grant now that this brutal business of war by sea and land may be lulled to rest. For you alone have power to give mortals the blessing of quiet peace. In your bosom Mars himself, supreme commander in this affairs of brutality, flings himself down at times, laid low by the irremediable wound of love. Gazing upward, his neck a prostrate column, fixing hungry eyes on you, great goddess, and gluts them with love.

As Mars lies outstretched, his breath hangs upon your lips.

Stoop, then, goddess most glorious, and enfold him at rest in your sacred bosom and whisper with those lips sweet words of prayer, imploring for the people of Rome restful peace.

In this evil hour of my country's history, I cannot do my task with a mind at ease, as an illustrious scion of the house of Memmius cannot at such a crisis halted his service from the common weal. I beg you for peace. Being that it is essential to the very nature of deity that it should enjoy existence in utter peace, aloof and detached from human affairs. Free it must be from all pain and peril, strong in its own resources, exempt from any need of us, unmoved to our merits and immune from anger.

My Memmius, lay aside your cares and lend undistracted ears and an attentive mind to true reason in what follows. Grasp before you scornfully reject the gifts I have garnered for you with zealous devotion. I will set out to speak to you on the ultimate realities of heaven and the gods.

2 — Dedication to Memmius

`I will explain those *atoms* from which nature creates all things and increases and feeds them and into which, when they perish, nature again restores them. To these in my speech I commonly give such names as the 'raw material', or 'generative bodies', or 'seeds' of things. Or I may call them 'original particles', because they come first and everything else is composed of them.

3 — On superstition

[Epicurus and religion] When human life lay crawling in all men's sight, crushed to the earth under the dead weight of *superstition* whose fierce features hovered menacingly upon mortals from the four quarters of the sky, a man of Greece[3] was first to raise defiant mortal eyes, standing erect to brave the challenge. Fables of the gods did not crush him, and less the lightning flash and the roaring menace of the sky, quickening, instead, keen courage of his heart, so that he, first of all men, longed to smash the hindering locks of nature's doors.

The vital power of his mind prevailed.

He ventured far out over the flaming ramparts of the world, voyaging in mind throughout infinity.

Returning victorious, he asserted what can be and what cannot: how the power of each thing is limited, and its boundaries of stone buried deep. Leaving superstition in its turn lying crushed beneath his feet, and we by his triumph are lifted level with the skies.

[The impiety of religion] What worries me is the fear that you may fancy yourself setting off on an impious course of philosophy and stepping on the path of sin.

Far from it.

[The example of Iphigenia's sacrifice] More often than not this very superstition is the mother of sinful and impious deeds. Remember how at Aulis[4] the altar of the virgin goddess was wickedly stained with the blood of Iphigenia by the commanders of the Greeks, the patterns of chivalry. The headband was placed about her virgin tresses, hanging down evenly over both of her cheeks.

Suddenly she caught sight of her father standing miserably in front of the altar, the aids beside him hiding the knife and her people bursting into tears when they saw her. Struck dumb with terror, she sank on her knees to the ground. Unfortunate girl, at such a moment it did not help her that she had been first to give the name of father to a king. Elevated by the hands of men, she was carried trembling to the altar; but not for her the sacrament of marriage and the loud chant of Hymen. It was her fate in the very hour of marriage to fall a sinless victim to a sinful rite, slaughtered to her greater grief by a father's hand, so that a fleet might sail under happy winds.

Such are the heights of wickedness to which men have been driven by superstition.

[The fear of death and its cure] If you yourself surrender your judgment at any time to the blood-curdling rants of the prophets, you will want to desert our ranks. Only think what ghosts they can conjure up to overturn the tenor of your life and wreck your happiness with fear.

And not without cause.

For, if men saw that a term was set to their troubles, they would find strength in some way to resist the hocus-pocus and threats of the prophets. As it is, they have no power to resist because they are haunted by the fear of eternal damnation after death, nothing of the nature of the spirit.

[Nature of the soul] Is the spirit born, or is it implanted in us at birth? Does it perish with us, dispersed by death, or does it move to the murky depths and dismal sloughs of the Underworld? Or is it transplanted by divine power into other beings, as described in the poems of our own Ennius,[5] who first gathered on the delectable slopes of mount Helicon an evergreen garland which was to win fame among the nations of Italy? As a matter of fact, Ennius in his immortal verses says that there is also a Hell, which is peopled not by our actual spirits or bodies but only by shadowy and ghastly pale images. It is from this realm that he pictures the ghost of Homer, of ever fresh memory, as appearing to him, crying salted tears and revealing the nature of the universe.

4 — The nature of the universe

I feel compelled to give an account of celestial phenomena, explaining the movements of sun and moon and also the forces that set events on earth. Next, and no less important, we must explore with keen insight into the make-up of spirit and mind; considering also those alarming phantasms that strike upon our minds when they are awake but made chaotic by sickness. Or when they are buried in slumber, so that we seem to see and hear before us men whose dead bones lie in the entrails of earth.

I am well aware that it is not easy to enlighten in Latin verse the obscure discoveries of the Greeks. The poverty of our language and the novelty of the theme often force me to coin new words for the purpose. But your merit and the joy I hope to derive from our joyful friendship heartens me to face any task however hard, leading me to stay awake through the quiet of the night, studying how by choice of words and the poet's art I can shine before your mind a clear light by which you can gaze into the heart of hidden things.

5 — First principle of nature

Only by grasping the outward form and inner workings of nature can we remove the dread and darkness of the mind: the sunbeams, shining shafts of day cannot. In tackling this theme, our starting-point will be this principle:

Nothing is ever created by divine power out of nothing.

The reason why all mortals are so seized by fear is that they see all sorts of things happening on the earth and in the sky with no obvious cause, thus attributing them to the will of a god. So, when we finally see that nothing can be created out of nothing, we shall then have a clearer picture of the path ahead, the problem of how things are created and caused without the aid of gods.

[All things require fixed seeds] First, if things were made out of nothing, any species could spring from any source and nothing would require seed. Men could spring from the sea and scaly fish from the earth, and birds could be hatched out of the sky. Cattle and other farm animals and every kind of wild beast, multiplying willy-nilly, would occupy tilled and waste lands alike. The same fruits would not grow repeatedly on the same trees, but they would keep changing, with any tree bearing any fruit. If each species were not constituted of its own generative bodies, why should each be born always of the same kind of mother?

[The result of fixed seeds is fixed substances] In fact, since each is formed out of specific seeds, each is born and emerges into the sunlit world only from a place where the right material exists—the right kind of atoms. This is why everything cannot be born of everything, but a unique power to generate inheres in specific objects.

[**Fixed seasons of birth also**] So, why do we see roses appear in spring, grain in summer's heat, grapes under the spell of autumn? Certainly, because only after specific seeds have drifted together at their own proper time does every created thing stand revealed; when the season is favorable, and the life-giving earth can safely deliver delicate growths into the sunlit world. If they were made out of nothing, they would sprout suddenly at random lapses of time and at abnormal seasons, since there would be no primary bodies that could be barred by the harshness of the season from entering into generative unions.

[**And fixed periods for increase**] Likewise, there would be no need of any lapse of time for the accumulation of seed in order that things might grow. Tiny tots would grow suddenly into young men, and trees would shoot up spontaneously out of the earth. Clearly none of these things happens since, as is natural, everything grows gradually from a specific seed, retaining its unique character. It is a fair inference that each is increased and nourished by its own raw material.

Furthermore, without seasonable showers the earth cannot send up gladdening growths; so, lacking food, animals cannot reproduce themselves or sustain life. From this we can conclude that many elements are common to many things, as letters are to words, rather than to the theory that anything can come into existence without atoms.

[**And fixed limit of growth**] Or again, why hasn't nature produced men on such a scale that they could ford the ocean on foot or tear down high mountains with their hands or prolong their lives over many generations?[6] Simply because each thing requires for its birth a particular matter that determines what can be produced. Let's admit that nothing can be made out of nothing because each thing must be generated from a seed before it can sprout into the unresisting air.

Lastly, we see that tilled plots are superior to untilled ones, and their fruits are improved by cultivation. This is because the earth contains certain atoms that we foster to productivity by turning the fruitful clods with the ploughshare and by stirring up the soil. But without these, would you would see great improvements arising spontaneously without any aid from our toil?

6 — The second principle of nature
The second great principle is this:
Nature resolves everything into its component atoms, never reducing anything to nothing.

If a thing were perishable in all its parts, the thing will perish all of a sudden, vanishing from sight. And there would be no need of any force to pull its parts and loosen their links. In actual fact, since everything is composed of indestructible seeds, nature does not allow anything to perish till it encounters a force that shatters it with a blow or creeps into chinks and unravels it.

If the things that are banished from the scene by age are ended through the exhaustion of their matter, from what source does then Venus bring back the several races of animals into the light of life? And, once they are brought back, from where does the inventive earth get for each the special food required for its sustenance and growth?

[The world could not be replenished] From what fount is the sea replenished by its native springs and the streams flowing into it from far away? From where does the ether draw nutriment for the stars? For everything consisting of a mortal body must have been used up by the long passage of time, the illimitable past. If along this bygone eternity bodies had persisted from which the universe has been perpetually renewed, they must surely possess immortality. Hence, things cannot be reduced to nothing.

Again, all objects would regularly be annihilated by the same force and the same cause, if it wasn't the case that they are sustained by imperishable matter more or less tightly fastened together.

Clearly, a mere touch would be enough to bring about

destruction if there were no imperishable bodies whose union could be dissolved only by the appropriate force. In fact, the fastenings of the atoms are of various kinds while their matter is imperishable. Compound objects remain whole until they encounter a force that proves strong enough to break up its particular constitution.

Therefore nothing returns to nothing, but everything is resolved into its constituent bodies.

[The loss of one thing appears as the gain of another] Lastly, showers perish when father ether flings them down into the lap of mother earth. But the crops spring up fresh; the branches on the trees burst into leaf; the trees grow and are weighed down with fruit. In turn man and beast draw nourishment. Hence, we see flourishing cities blessed with children and every leafy thicket loud with new broods of songsters. Hence in lush pastures cattle weighed by their bulk fling down their bodies, the white milky juice oozing from their swollen udders. Hence a new breed frolics friskily on wobbly legs through the fresh grass, their young minds tipsy with undiluted milk.

Visible objects therefore do not totally perish because nature repairs one thing from another, allowing nothing to be born without the aid of another's death.

7 — About Atoms

[Invisible things exist supported by other invisible bodies] Well, Memmius, I have taught you that things cannot be created out of nothing nor, once born, be called back to nothing. Possibly, you are becoming mistrustful of my words, because these atoms of mine are not visible to the eye.

Consider, therefore, this further evidence of bodies whose existence you must acknowledge though they cannot be seen.

First, wind, when its force is roused, it whips up waves, sinks tall ships and scatters clouds; sometimes by scouring plains with hurricane force it strews them with huge trees and batters mountain peaks with blasts that cut down forests. Such is wind in its fury, when it whoops aloud with a mad menace in its roaring. Without doubt, therefore, there must be invisible particles of wind that sweep sea, that sweep land, that sweep the clouds in the sky, swooping upon them and whirling them along in a reckless hurricane.

In the way they flow and the chaos they spread they are no different from a torrential flood of water when it rushes down in a sudden spate from the mountain heights, swollen by heavy rains, heaping together wreckage from the forest and entire trees. Soft though it is by nature, the sudden shock of oncoming water is more than even stout bridges can withstand. Furious is the force with which the turbid, storm-flushed torrent surges against their piers. With a mighty roar it lays them low, rolling huge rocks under its waves and brushing aside every obstacle from its course. Likewise the movement of blasts of wind.

When they come surging along some course like a rushing river, they push obstacles before them and buffet them with repeated blows; and sometimes, eddying round and round, they snatch them up and carry them along in a swiftly circling vortex. Here then is proof upon proof that winds have invisible bodies, since in their actions and behavior they rival great rivers, whose bodies are plain and visible.

Also, we smell the various scents of things though we never see them near our nostrils. Similarly, we do not look upon scorching heat nor can we grasp cold in our eyes and we do not see sounds. Yet all these must be composed of physical bodies, since they are able to register upon our senses. For nothing can touch or be touched except bodies.

Again, clothes hanging on a surf-beaten shore grow moist. When spread in the sun they grow dry. But we do not see how the moisture soaks into them, or how it is dispelled by the heat. It follows that the moisture is split up into minute parts which the eye cannot possibly see.

[The evidence of decay] Again, in the course of many annual revolutions of the sun a finger ring is worn thin with continual rubbing. Dripping water hollows a stone. A curved ploughshare, iron though it is, dwindles imperceptibly in the furrow. In highways we see the cobblestones worn out by the feet of many wayfarers. The bronze statues by the city gates show their right hands worn thin by the touch of travelers who greet them in passing. Obviously, all these things are being diminished, since they are worn away. But to perceive what particles drop off at any particular time is a power denied to us by our ungenerous sense of sight.

To sum up, what is added to things gradually by nature and the passage of time, causing a cumulative increase, eludes the most attentive scrutiny of our eyes. Conversely, you cannot see what objects lose by the wastage of age —sheer sea cliffs, for instance, exposed to prolonged erosion by the biting brine— or at what time the loss occurs.

It follows that nature works through the agency of invisible bodies.

8 — Vacuity

On the other hand, things are not hemmed in by the pressure of solid bodies in a tight mass. This is because there is empty space in things. A grasp of this fact will be helpful to you in many respects and will save you from much baffling doubt and questioning about the universe and from mistrust of my teaching.

Well then, by vacuity I mean intangible and empty space.

[No motion without void] If space did not exist, things could not move at all. For the distinctive action of matter, which is counteraction and obstruction, would be in force always and everywhere. Nothing could move forward, because nothing would give it a starting-point by receding. But we see with our eyes at sea and on land and high up in the sky that all sorts of things in all sorts of ways are on the move. If there were no empty space, these things would be denied the power of restless movement, or rather: they could not possibly have come into existence, embedded as they would have been in motionless matter.

In addition, there are clear signs that things that pass for solid are in fact porous. Even in rocky caves a trickle of water seeps through, and every surface weeps with brimming drops.

Food percolates to every part of an animal's body. Trees grow and yield their fruit in season, because their food circulates throughout their length from the tips of the roots through the trunk and along every branch. Noises pass through walls, flying into closed buildings. Freezing cold penetrates to the bones.

If there were no empty spaces through which the various bodies could make their way, none of these phenomena would be possible.

Again, why do we find some things outweigh others of equal volume? If there is as much matter in a ball of wool as in one of lead, it is natural that it should weigh as heavily, since it is the function of matter to push everything downwards, while it is the function of space on the other hand to remain weightless. So, when one thing is not less bulky than another but obviously lighter, it plainly tells that there is more vacuum in it, while the heavier object proclaims that there is more matter in it and much less empty space.

We have now reached the goal of our diligent enquiry: there is in things an admixture of what we call *vacuity*.

[The false theory of motion without void] Should you should be misled on this question by the idle imagining of certain theorists, I must anticipate their argument. They hold that water yields and opens up liquid ways to the scaly bodies of fish that push against it, because they leave spaces behind them into which the yielding water can flow together. In the same way, they suppose, other things can move by mutually changing places, despite the fact that every place remains filled. This theory has been adopted totally without justification. For how can the fish advance till the water has given way? And how can the water retire when the fish cannot move? There are thus only two alternatives: either all bodies are devoid of movement, or you must admit that things contain an admixture of vacuity whereby each is enabled to make the first move.

[Things don't move without room to move about] Lastly, if two broad bodies suddenly spring apart from contact, all the intervening space must be void until it is occupied by air. Regardless of quickly the air rushes in all around, the entire space cannot be filled instantaneously. The air must occupy one spot after another until it has taken possession of the whole space. If anyone believes that this consequence of such springing apart is made possible by the condensation of air, he is mistaken. Condensation implies that something that was full becomes empty, or vice versa. And I hold that air could not condense so as to produce this effect; or, at any rate, if there were no vacuum, it could not thus shrink into itself and draw its parts together.

However many pleas you may advance to prolong the argument, you must end by admitting that there is vacuity in things.

I could scrape together many other proofs and add them into the pile to strengthen conviction; but for an acute intelligence these small clues should suffice so that you can discover the rest for yourself.

As hounds often smell out the lairs of a mountain-ranging quarry camouflaged in thickets, when once they have got on to the right trail, so in such questioning one thing will lead on to another, till you can succeed by yourself in tracking down the truth to its lurking places and drag it out. If you tire and relax from the chase, there is one thing, Memmius, that I can safely promise you: my honeyed tongue will pour from the treasury of my breast such generous draughts, drawn from inexhaustible springs, that I am afraid slow plodding age may creep through my limbs, unbolting the bars of my life before the full flood of my arguments on any single point has flowed in verse through your ears.

9 — Bodies and vacant space

[The two natures: matter and void] To pick up the thread of my discourse, all nature as it is in itself consists of two things: bodies and the vacant space where the bodies are situated and moving in different directions.

The existence of bodies is proven by the agreement of the senses. If a belief resting directly on this foundation isn't valid, there will be no standard to which we can refer any doubt on obscure questions for rational confirmation. If there were no place and space —which we call vacuity— these bodies could not be located anywhere or move in any direction whatever. This I have just demonstrated.

It remains to show that:

Nothing exists that is distinct both from body and from vacuity.

We could rank this with the others as a third substance. For whatever *is* must also be something. If it offers resistance to touch, whether light and slight, it will increase the mass of body by such amount, great or small, as it may amount to, and will rank with it. If, in contrast, it is intangible, so that it offers no resistance whatever to anything passing through it, then it will be that empty space which we call vacuity.

[No third nature exists] So, this thing in itself, either it acts in some way, or reacts to other things acting upon it, or else it will be such that things can be and happen within it. But without body nothing can act or react; and nothing can afford a place except emptiness and vacancy. Consequently, other than *matter* and *vacuity*, we cannot count among the number of things any third substance to either affect our senses at any time or be grasped by the reasoning of our minds.

10 — Property, accidents, and time

You will find that a thing that can be named is either a property or an accident of these two. A *property* being something that cannot be detached or split from a thing without destroying it: such as weight is a property of rocks, heat of fire, fluidity of water, tangibility of all bodies, intangibility of vacuum. On the other hand, servitude, poverty and riches, freedom, war, peace and all other things whose presence or departure leaves the essence of a thing intact, all these we shall call by their appropriate name: *accidents*.

[Time is not a separate existence, but an accident of things] In the same vein, *time* by itself does not exist; but from things themselves there results a sense of what has already taken place, what is now going on and what will ensue.

No one may claim that can sense time by itself apart from the movement of things or their restful immobility.

[False argument from past events] Again, when men say it *is* a fact that Helen was ravished or the Trojans were conquered, we must not let anyone drive us to admit that any such factual event *exists* independently of any object, on the ground that the generations of people of whom these events were accidents have been swept away by the irrevocable lapse of time. We could put it that whatever has taken place is an accident of a specific tract of earth or of the space it occupied.

Had there been no matter and no space or place in which things could happen, no spark of love kindled by the beauty of Tyndareus' daughter[7] would ever have glowed inside the breast of Phrygian Paris to light that dazzling blaze of that pitiless war. No Wooden Horse, undetected by the sons of Troy, would have set the towers of Ilium aflame through the midnight, as Greeks issued from its womb.

[Without matter and space events cannot exists] So you may see that events cannot be said to *be* by themselves like matter or in the same sense as space. Instead, you should describe them as accidents of matter, or of the place in which things happen.

11 — Atoms and compounds

Material objects are of two kinds:
Atoms and compounds of atoms.

The atoms cannot be cracked by any force, for they are preserved indefinitely by their absolute solidity. It is hard to admit that anything can exist that is absolutely solid. The lightning stroke from the sky penetrates closed buildings, as well as shouts and other noises. Iron glows white-hot in the fire, and rocks crack in savage scorching heat. Hard gold is softened and melted by heat; and the ice of bronze is liquefied by flame. Both heat and piercing cold seep through silver, since we feel both when a cooling shower of water is poured into a goblet that we hold ceremonially in our hands. All these facts signal that nothing is really solid.

Yet sound reasoning and nature itself drive us to the opposite conclusion.

So, pay attention while I demonstrate in a few lines that certain bodies exist that are absolutely solid and indestructible, namely those atoms which according to our teaching are the seeds of prime units of things from which the whole universe is built up.

[Void and body are mutually exclusive] We have found that nature is twofold, consisting of two totally different things, *matter and the space* in which things happen. Hence each of these must exist by itself without admixture of the other. For, where there is empty space (what we call vacuity), matter is absent; where matter exists, there cannot be a vacuum. Therefore the prime units of matter are solid and free from vacuity.

Since compound things contain some vacuum, the surrounding matter must be solid. You cannot logically maintain that a thing can hide vacuity, holding it within its body unless you allow that the container itself is solid. And what holds the vacuum in things can only be an accumulation of matter. Hence matter, which possesses absolute solidity, can be everlasting when other things are decomposed.

Again, if there were no empty space, everything would be one solid mass; if there were no material objects with the property of filling the space they occupy, all existing space would be utterly void. Obviously, then, that there is an alternation of matter and vacuity, mutually distinct, since the whole is neither completely full nor completely empty.

[Some solid bodies cannot be broken and are therefore

eternal] There exist therefore solid bodies, causing the distinction between empty space and full. And these, as I have just shown, can be neither decomposed by blows from without nor invaded and unraveled from within nor destroyed by any other form of assault. For it seems that a thing without vacuum can be neither knocked to bits nor snapped nor chopped in two by cutting; nor can it let in moisture or seeping cold or piercing fire, the universal agents of destruction. The more vacuum a thing contains within it, the more readily it yields to these assailants.

It follows then, if the units of matter are solid and without vacuity, as I have shown, they must be indestructible.

Yet again, if the matter in things wasn't indestructible, everything by now would have gone back to nothing, and the things we see would be the product of rebirth out of nothing. But, since I have already shown that nothing can be created out of nothing nor any existing thing be summoned back to nothing, the *atoms* must be made of indestructible stuff into which everything can be resolved in the end, so that there may be a stock of matter for building the world anew.

Clearly then, atoms are absolutely solid and unalloyed. In no other way could they have survived throughout infinite time to keep the world renewed.

[Without limit to division there's no maturity] Besides, if nature had set no limit to the breaking of things, the particles of matter in the course of ages would have been crushed so small that nothing could be generated from them so as to attain from them in the fullness of time to the summit of its growth. For we see that anything can be more speedily disintegrated than put together again. Hence, what the long passage of time, the bygone eternity, has already shaken and loosened to fragments could never in the residue of time be reconstructed.

As things are, there is evidently a limit set to breaking, since we see that everything is renewed and each according to its kind has a fixed period in which to grow to its prime.

[Solid bodies with void can make soft things; the

reverse is impossible] Let's look at a further argument. Granted that the particles of matter are absolutely solid, we can still explain the composition and behavior of soft things —air, water, earth, fire—[8] by their intermixture with empty space. On the other hand, supposing the atoms to be soft, we cannot account for the origin of hard flint and iron, and there would be no foundation for nature to build on. Consequently, there must be bodies strong in their unalloyed solidity by whose closer clustering things can be knit together and display unyielding toughness.

If we suppose that there is no limit set to the breaking of matter, we must still admit that material objects consist of particles which throughout eternity have survived the forces of destruction. To say that these particles are breakable does not square with the fact that they have survived throughout eternity under perennial bombardment.

[Eternal atoms account for the persistence of species] Again, there is laid down for each thing a specific limit to its growth and its tenure of life, the laws of nature ordaining what each can do and what it cannot. No species ever changes, remaining so much itself that every kind of *bird* displays on its body its own specific features. This is a further proof that their bodies are made of changeless matter. Now, if the atoms could submit in any way to change, there would be no certainty as to what could arise and what could not, at what point the power of everything was limited by an immovable frontier post; nor could successive generations so regularly repeat the nature, behavior, habits and movements of their parents.

To go on with our argument, there is an ultimate point in visible objects that represents the smallest thing that can be seen. So also there must be an ultimate point in objects that lie below the limit of perception by our senses. This point is without parts and is the smallest thing that can exist. It never has been and never will be able to exist alone, but only as one primary part of something else. It is with a mass of such parts, solidly jammed together information, that matter is filled up.

Since these primary parts cannot exist by themselves, they must need stick together in a mass from which they cannot by any means be prized loose.

The atoms, then, are absolutely solid and unalloyed, consisting of a mass of least parts tightly packed together. They are not compounds formed by the heaping of their parts, but bodies of absolute and everlasting solidity. To these nature allows no loss or diminution, guarding them as seeds for things. If there are no such least parts, even the smallest bodies consist of an infinite number of parts, since they can always be halved and their halves halved again without limit. On this showing, what difference will there be between the whole universe and the very least of things? None at all. As boundless and infinite the universe may be, yet the smallest things will equally consist of an infinite number of parts. Since true reason cries out against this and denies that the mind can believe it, you need to give in and admit that there are least parts which themselves are partless. Granted that these parts exist, you need to admit that the atoms they compose are also solid and everlasting. But, if all things were compelled by all-creating nature to be broken up into these least parts, nature would lack the power to rebuild anything out of them. Partless objects cannot have the essential properties of generative matter: those varieties of attachment, weight, impetus, impact and movement on which everything depends.

12 — Heraclitus' theory

For all these reasons: *those who imagine that the raw material of things is fire and the universe consists of fire alone have evidently wandered far from the truth.*

Of these the first champion to plunge into the fray was Heraclitus,[9] illustrious for the darkness of his speech, though rather among the lighter-witted of the Greeks than among those who are earnest seekers after truth. For fools are more impressed and intrigued by what they detect under a screen of riddling words, and accept as true what pleasantly tickles their ears and all that is dyed with a smart sound.

[Fire doesn't account for the variety of things] I should like to know how things can be so variegated if they are created out of nothing but sheer fire. It would not help if hot fire were condensed or rarefied, so long as the particles of fire retained the same nature that fire possesses as a whole. Its heat would simply be fiercer as its parts were more concentrated, milder as they were dispersed and dissipated. There is no further effect that you could attribute to such causes, no possibility that the infinite variety of things could result from variations in the density or rarity of fire.

Even these variations in density could not occur unless we allow in things an intermixture of vacuity. Seeing that many things run counter to their ideas, these theorists dodge the issue, declining to permit any pure vacuum in things. Shunning the steep, they lose the true path. They do not see that without vacuity everything would be condensed and would become one body, which could not throw off anything at high speed from itself as blazing fire throws off light and heat, which enables you to see that its parts are not solidly compacted.

[Fire ever changing to other things means ultimate destruction] On the other hand, if they think that there is some other way in which fires in combination can be quenched and change their substance, then obviously —if they do not shrink from any implication of this view— the fieriness must be completely annihilated and whatever emerges must be a new creation out of nothing.

If ever a thing is so transformed as to go beyond its own limits, this means the immediate death of what was before. It follows that they must leave something intact, or you would find everything reduced to nothing and the stock of things reborn and renewed from nothing.

[The true atomic view] As it is, there are certain definite bodies that always hold the same nature, and it is by the withdrawal or advent of these and their reshuffling that things change their nature and material objects are transformed. And these primary bodies cannot be fiery. So long as they possessed and retained a fiery nature, it would make no odds if some of them were detached and withdrawn and others tacked on and some were reshuffled. Whatever they created would still be simply fire.

The truth, as I maintain, is this:

Indeed, certain bodies whose impacts, movements, order, position and shapes produce fires. When their order is changed, they change their nature. In themselves they do not resemble fire or anything else that can bombard our senses with particles or impinge on our organs of touch.

To say, as Heraclitus does, that everything is fire, and nothing can be numbered among things as a reality except fire, seems rather crazy. On the basis of the senses he attacks and unsettles the senses, which are the foundation of all belief and the only source of his knowledge of that which he calls fire. He believes that the senses clearly perceive fire, but not the other things that are in fact no less clear, which strikes me as not only pointless but insane.

What is to be our standard of reference?

What can be a surer guide to the distinction of true from false than our own senses? What grounds have we for taking everything else and leaving fire, any more than for taking away everything else and leaving some other thing?

Either procedure appears equally insane.

For this reason those who have thought that fire is the raw material of things and the universe can consist of fire and those who have made *air*[10] the starting-point for the growth of things or have supposed that *water*[11] by itself could form everything or that *earth* could create all things and be transformed into their natures—all these have evidently strayed far from the truth.

Equally mistaken are those who make the elements two-fold, coupling air with fire and earth with water, and those who think that everything can grow from four elements, fire and earth and air and rain. Head over shoulders among these is **Empedodes of Acragas**, born in the three-cornered confines of that Isle round which laps the Ionian deep, rushing far into creeks and dashing up salt spray from its grey-green billows. The sea that parts it from Aeolian shores runs headlong through its narrow channel, where deadly Charybdis is, where the rumbling of Etna's flames is a warning that it is rallying its wrath that once again its force may spew out fires bursting in a torrent from its throat, to bring its flashing flames back up to the sky. This great country is known to have many claims to the admiration of mankind and the attention of sight-seekers. But, for all its surfeit of good things and its ample garrison of men, it has surely held nothing more glorious than this man, nothing holier, nothing more prodigious, nothing more precious. Indeed, the songs that took shape in his divine breast declare in ringing tones such glorious discoveries that he scarcely seems a scion of mortal stock. Empedocles and those lesser men of whom we have spoken above, ranking far and way below him, have certainly made many excellent and divine discoveries and uttered oracles from the inner sanctuary of their hearts with more sanctity and far surer reason than those the Delphic prophetess pronounces, drugged by the laurel fumes, from Apollo's tripod.

[Errors of Empedocles and his school] Yet among the very foundations of things they have come to grief. Great as they were, great has been their fall.

[They deny the void] Their first error is this: they postulate movement while banishing empty space from the universe, admitting the existence of soft and flimsy things: air, sun, water, earth, animals, vegetables, without allowing their bodies an intermixture of vacuity.

[They set no limit to division] Their second error: they acknowledge no limit to the splitting of things, no rest from crumbling, no smallest unit of matter, although we see that every object has an ultimate point that seems to our senses to be the smallest, from which you may infer that the things you cannot perceive have also an ultimate point which actually is the smallest.

Besides, since they rank as elements soft things that we

perceive to be neither birthless nor deathless, the universe ought by now to have returned to nothing and whatever exists ought to be a new creation and growth out of nothing, both of which suppositions you already know to be false. In addition, these so-named elements are in many ways hurtful and lethal to one another, so that they will either be destroyed on contact or will rush apart, as when a storm has gathered we see lightning flashes, rainclouds and winds rush apart.

Again, if everything is created from four things and resolved into them, why should we say that these are the elements of things rather than the reverse; that other things are the elements of these? One would then give birth to another continually, interchanging their colors and their entire natures throughout the whole of time. If, on the other hand, you believe that particles of fire and earth, airy wind and watery moisture, combine without changing their natures in combination, then nothing can be created from them, either animate or (like a tree) with inanimate body. For each element in a compound assemblage will betray its own nature; air will appear mixed with earth, and fire will remain side by side with moisture. But in fact the elements, in giving birth to things, must contribute a neutral nature that is hidden and invisible, so that nothing may show that conflicts with the thing created and prevents it from being distinctively itself.

These authors trace everything back to the sky and its fires. First they make fire transform itself into the winds of air; hence is born rain, and from rain is created earth. Then the process is reversed: first from earth is born moisture, then comes air, then fire. And things never cease to interchange, migrating from heaven to earth, from earth to the starry firmament. Yet this is something elements ought never to do. For it is essential that something should remain immutable, or everything would be reduced to nothing.

If ever anything is so transformed that it oversteps its own limits, this means the immediate death of what was before. Therefore, since the substances just mentioned enter into interchange, they must need to consist of other substances that cannot be altered, so that you may not find everything reduced to nothing. You ought rather to postulate bodies possessed of such a nature that, if they happen to have created fire, they only need a few subtractions and additions and some change of order and movement to make gusty air. In this way we can account for any change from one thing to another.

[Argument from the presence of the four elements in growth] "But," you say, "observation clearly shows that all growing things do grow up into the gusty air out of the earth and it is from the earth that they draw their food. And, unless an auspicious season gives free play to the rain, so that trees reel beneath the dissolving clouds, and unless the sun in turn provides favoring warmth, there can be no growth of crops, trees, or animals."

Yes, and unless we ourselves were sustained by dry food and fluid juices, our bodies would waste away till every bit of life had left from all our sinews and bones.

[The true atomic explanation] Doubtless, we are fed and nourished by certain specific things, other things by others, and so forth. Obviously, it is because there are in things many elements common to many commingled in many ways that various things draw their food from various sources. It often makes a big difference in what combinations and positions these elements occur, and what motions they mutually pass on or take over. For the same elements compose sky, sea and lands, rivers and sun, crops, trees and animals, but they are moving differently and in different combinations.

Consider how in my verses, for instance, you see many letters common to many words; yet you must admit that different verses and words differ in substance and in audible sound. So much can be done by letters through mere change of order. But the elements can bring more factors into play so as to create things in all their variety.

[Anaxagoras] Now let's examine Anaxagoras' theory,[12] which the Greeks call *homoeomeria:* the poverty of our native language will not let me translate the word, but the thing itself can be expressed easily enough. In speaking of the *homoeomeria* of things Anaxagoras means that bones are formed of minute miniature bones, flesh of minute miniature morsels of flesh, blood by the coalescence of many drops of blood; gold consists of grains of gold; earth is a conglomeration of little earths, fire of fires, moisture of moistures.

He pictures everything else as formed in the same way.

[He denies the void] At the same time he does not admit any vacuum in things, or any limit to the splitting of matter, on both of which counts he seems to me guilty of the same error as the others. Add to this that he makes the elements too weak, if indeed we can allow the name of 'elements' to bodies that have the same nature as the things themselves, that suffer and decay no less than they do and are not reined in by any force in their race to destruction.

Which of these weak things will withstand violent assault, so as to escape extinction in the very jaws of death? Will fire or water or air? Which of these? Blood or bones? Nothing, I maintain, will escape, where everything is as perishable as those objects that we see vanishing from before our eyes under stress of some force or other.

In proof of the impossibility of such annihilation and regrowth from nothing, I appeal to the evidence already produced.

Let's try again: since food builds up and nourishes our bodies, our veins and bones and blood and sinews must be composed of matter unlike themselves.

Alternatively, if it is alleged that all foods are of mixed substance and contain little morsels of sinews and bones and veins and drops of blood, it must be supposed that all food, whether solid or fluid, consists of unlike matter, namely of a mixture of bones and sinews, pus and blood. Similarly, if the material of all the things that grow out of the earth occurs in the earth, earth must consist of unlike matter that rises out of it.

Turning to other phenomena we see the same words will

hold good. If flame, smoke and ashes lurk unseen in wood, then wood must consist of unlike matter that rises out of it. Furthermore, all the material atoms that the earth feeds and makes to grow must consist of things unlike themselves, and they in turn must also contain things unlike themselves.

[**Anaxagoras' evasion**] But some scanty cover for escaping detection exists, and Anaxagoras avails himself of it. He asserts that there is in everything a mixture of everything, but all the ingredients escape detection except the one whose particles are most numerous and conspicuous and stand in the front line. This is far removed from the truth. Otherwise it would naturally happen that corn, when it is crushed by the dire force of the grindstone, would often show some trace of blood, and that blood would exude when we crush between stones any of those things that derive material from our bodies.

Similarly, grass and water ought often to emit sweet drops of the same flavor as the milk in the udders of fleecy ewes. When clods of soil are crumbled, finely divided particles of different plants and grains and leaves ought to become visible, lurking among the soil. When sticks are snapped, ashes and smoke ought to be exposed and tiny hidden fires.

But observation clearly shows that nothing of the kind happens.

Consequently, one sort of thing is not intermingled with another in this way, but there must be in things a mixture of invisible seeds that are common to many sorts.

[**Argument from forest conflagrations**] "But," you may object, "it often happens in mountainous country that the tops of tall trees rub together by the force of strong south winds till suddenly they explode into a blaze of flame." Agreed. And yet there is no fire embedded in the wood. What it does contain is a multitude of seeds of heat, which start a conflagration in the forest only when they have been concentrated by rubbing. If there were ready-made flame concealed in the wood, the fires could not be hidden for any length of time; they would spread chaos through the woodland, burning the trees to ashes.

Now do you see the point of my previous remark, that it makes a great difference in what combinations and positions the same elements occur and what motions they mutually pass on and take over, so that with a little reshuffling they produce forests and fires? This is just how the words themselves are formed, by a little reshuffling of the letters, when we pronounce 'forests' and 'fires' as two distinct utterances.

[Reduction ad absurdum] If you cannot account for what you see happen without inventing particles of matter with the same sort of nature as the whole objects, there is an end of your elements altogether. You might as well postulate particles that shake their sides with ridiculous guffaws, begriming their cheeks with salt tears.

13 — My poetry and my reward

[Lucretius; man on a mission] And now heed what follows and listen more intently. I am well aware how full it is of obscurity. But high hope of fame has struck my heart with its holy staff and in so doing has implanted in my breast the sweet love of the Muses. That is the spur that lends my spirit strength to pioneer through new paths of their Pierian realm where no foot has ever trod before. What joy it is to light upon virgin springs and drink their waters. What joy to pluck new flowers and gather for my brow a glorious garland from fields whose blossoms were never yet wreathed by the Muses round any head.

This is my reward for teaching on these lofty topics, for struggling to loose men's minds from the tight knots of superstition and shining on dark material the bright beams of my song that irradiate everything with the sparkle of the Muses.

But my art is not without a purpose.

Physicians, when they wish to treat children with a nasty dose of wormwood, first smear the rim of the cup with the sweet yellow fluid of honey. The children, too young as yet for foresight, are lured by the sweetness at their lips into swallowing the bitter medicine. So they are tricked but not trapped, for the medicine restores them to health. Likewise, our doctrine often seems unpalatable to those who have not handled it, and the masses shrink from it. That is why I have tried to administer my philosophy to you in the dulcet strains of poetry, to touch it with the sweet honey of the Muses. My object has been to engage your mind with my verses while you gain insight into the nature of the universe and the pattern of its architecture.

[**Infinity**] All right, since I have shown that there are completely solid indestructible particles of matter flying about through all eternity, let us unroll whether or not there is any limit to their number. Similarly, as we have found that there is a vacuum, the place or space in which things happen, let us see whether its whole extent is limited or whether it stretches far and wide into boundless depths.

14 — The boundless universe

Learn, therefore, that:

The universe is not bounded in any direction.

If it were, it would need to have a limit somewhere. But we know a thing cannot have a limit unless there is something outside to limit it, so that the eye can follow it up to a certain point but not beyond.

Since you must admit that there is nothing outside the universe, it can have no limit, and it is thus without end or measure. It doesn't matter in which part of it you may take your stand: whatever spot anyone may occupy, the universe stretches away from him just the same in all directions without limit.

[**An experiment with a dart**] Assume for an instant that the whole of space were bounded and that someone made his way to its uttermost boundary and threw a flying dart. Do you choose to think that the missile, hurled with might, would speed along the trajectory on which it was aimed? Or do you think something would block the way, stopping it? You must assume one alternative or the other. But neither of them leaves you a loophole. Both force you to admit that the universe continues without end. Whether there is some obstacle lying on the boundary line that prevents the dart from going farther on its course or whether it flies on beyond, it cannot in fact have started from the boundary. With this argument I will pursue you. Wherever you may place the ultimate limit of things, I will ask you: "Well then, what does happen to the dart?"

The result is that the boundary cannot stand firm anywhere, and final escape from this conclusion is precluded by the limitless possibility of running away from it.

Besides, if all the space in the universe were shut in and confined on every side by definite boundaries, the supply of matter would already have accumulated by its own weight at the bottom, and nothing could happen under the dome of the sky; indeed, there would be no sky and no sunlight, since all the available matter would have settled down and would be lying in a heap for all eternity.

The truth is, no rest is given to the atoms, because there is no bottom where they can accumulate and take up their abode.

Things go on happening all the time through endless motion in every direction; and atoms of matter bouncing up from below are supplied out of the infinite.

[The sensible world] Finally, by observation we prove that one thing is limited by another. The hills are demarcated by air, and air by the hills; land sets bounds to sea, and sea to every land. But the universe has nothing outside to limit it. Hence, there's only a limitless abyss of space that even the dazzling flashes of the lightning cannot traverse it in their course, racing through an interminable tract of time, nor can they even shorten the distance still to be covered; so vast is the span that lies open to things far and wide without limit in any dimension.

The universe is refrained from setting any limit to itself by nature, which compels body to be bounded by vacuum and vacuum by body. Thus nature either makes them both infinite in alternation, or else one of them, if it is not bounded by the other, must extend in a pure state without limit. Space, however, being infinite, so must matter be. Or, neither sea nor land nor the bright zones of the sky nor mortal beings nor the holy bodies of the gods could endure for one brief hour of time.

The supply of matter would be shaken loose from combination and swept through the vastness of the void in individual particles. Better yet, matter would never have coalesced to form anything, since its scattered particles could never have been driven into union.

[The world was not formed by design but by chance] The atoms did not accommodate themselves in due order and deliberately by an act of intelligent design, nor did they stipulate what movements each should perform. As they have been rushing forever throughout all space in their myriads, undergoing a myriad changes under the disturbing impact of collisions, they have experienced every sort of movement and union till they have fallen into the particular pattern by which this world of ours is constituted.

Once the world was set going with the proper motions, it has persisted many a long year, with everything else following: the rivers replenish the thirsty sea with profuse streams of water. Warmed by the sun's heat, the earth renews its fruits, and the brood of animals that spawns from it grows lustily, with the gliding fires of ether sustaining their life. None of these things would be possible if there were not an ample supply of matter to bounce up out of infinite space to replace all that is lost.

Just as animals deprived of food waste away through loss of body, so everything must decay as soon as its supply of matter goes astray and is cut off.

Whatever world the atoms combine to form, impacts from without cannot preserve it at every point because by continual battering they can only hold back part of it till others come along to make good the deficiency. But they are forced now and then to bounce back, leaving ample space and time for the atoms to break free from combination. Hence, it is essential that there should be great numbers of atoms coming up.

Indeed, the impacts themselves could not be maintained without an unlimited supply of matter from all direction.

[False theory of the Stoics] There is one belief, Memmius, that you must beware of entertaining: *the theory that everything tends towards what they call "the center of the universe."* On this centripetal theory, the world stands fixed, without any impacts from without; and top and bottom cannot be parted in any direction because everything has been tending towards the center. If you can believe that anything rests upon itself. Whatever heavy bodies there may be under the earth must then tend upwards and rest against the surface upside down, like the images of things which we now see reflected in water.

[Absurdities] In the same way they would have it that animals walk about chaotically and cannot fall off the earth into the nether quarters of the sky any more than our bodies can soar up spontaneously into the heavenly regions. When they are looking at the sun, they see the stars of night which share the hours with us alternately and experience nights corresponding to our days.

But this is an idle fancy of fools who have got hold of the wrong end of the stick.

There can be no center in infinity.

And, even if there were, nothing could stand still there rather than flee from it. For all place or space, at the center no less than elsewhere, must give way to heavy bodies, regardless of what direction they are moving. There is no place to which bodies can come where they lose the property of weight and stand still in the void. Since vacuum cannot support anything but rather must allow it free passage, as its own nature demands, so, things cannot be held in combination by this means through surrender to a craving for the center.

[Inconsistencies] Besides, they do not claim that all bodies have this tendency towards the center, but only those of moisture and earth: the waters of the deep, the floods that pour down from the hills and in general whatever is composed of a more or less earthy body. Yet, they teach that the light breaths of air and hot fires are simultaneously wafted outwards away from the center. The reason why the encircling ether twinkles with stars and the sun feeds its flames in the blue pastures of the sky is that fire congregates there in its flight from the center. And along the same line: the topmost branches of trees could not break into leaf unless their food had this same upward urge. But, if you allow matter to escape from the world in this way, you are leaving the walls of the world at liberty to crumble suddenly, taking flight with the speed of flame into the boundless void.

The rest will then follow.

The thunder-breeding quarters of the sky will rush down from up above. The ground will fall away from under our feet, and its particles dissolved amid the mingled wreckage of heaven and earth. The whole world will vanish into the abyss, and in the twinkling of an eye nothing will be left but empty space and invisible atoms.

[Without infinite matter the world would be destroyed]
At whatever point you first allow matter to fall short, this will be the gateway to perdition, and through this gateway the whole concourse of matter will come streaming out.

If you take a little trouble, you will attain to a thorough grasp of these truths, with one thing illuminating the other, so that eyeless night will not rob you of your path till you have looked into the heart of nature's darkest mysteries. So surely will facts throw light upon facts.

BOOK TWO — MOVEMENTS AND S[HAPES] OF ATOMS

15 — Body and mind

When out at sea the storm winds are lashing the waters, and gazing from the shore at the heavy stress some other man is enduring—what joy we feel!

Not that anyone's sufferings are in themselves a source of delight; the fact of the matter is that in realizing how free we are from troubles we are filled with joy indeed.

Once again, what joy it is to watch opposing forces gathered on the field of battle when you have yourself no part in their peril! But this is the greatest joy of all: to own a quiet sanctuary, stoutly fortified by the teaching of the wise, and from that lofty spot to gaze on others wandering aimlessly in search of a way of life, pitting their wits one against another, disputing for precedence, struggling night and day with lavish effort to climb the heights of wealth and power.

Oh joyless hearts of men! Oh mind without vision! How dark and dangerous the life in which this tiny span is lived away!

Do you not see that nature calls for two things only: a body free from pain, and a mind released from worry and fear for the enjoyment of pleasurable sensations?

[Body needs are few] So we find that our bodily nature requirements are *few* indeed, no more than is necessary to banish pain, and also to spread out many pleasures for ourselves. Nature does not periodically seek anything more pleasing than this, never complaining whether golden images of youths about the house, hold flaming torches in their hands to illuminate banquets prolonged into the night.

Does it matter if the hall does not sparkle with silver and gleam with gold, and no carved and gilded rafters ring to the music of the lute?

Nature does not miss these luxuries when men recline in company on the soft grass by a running stream under the branches of a tall tree, refreshing their bodies pleasurably at small expense. Better still if the weather smiles upon them, and the season of the year crowns the green herbage with flowers. Burning fevers flee no swifter from your body if you toss under carved counterpanes and coverlets of crimson than if you must lie in rude homespun cloth.

If our bodies are not profited by treasures or tides or the glories of kingship, we must go on to admit that neither our minds gain from them.

Or tell me, Memmius, when you see your legions thronging Mars' Campus in the ardor of drill warfare, supported by ample auxiliaries and a force of cavalry, gorgeously armed and fired by a common purpose, does that sight scare the terrors of superstition from your mind? Does the fear of death flee from your breast, leaving it carefree? Or do we not find such resources absurdly useless? The fears and anxieties that plague the human breast do not shrink from the clash of arms or the fierce rain of missiles; they stalk unabashed among princes and potentates; they are not awestruck by the gleam of gold or the bright sheen of purple robes.

Can you doubt then that this power rests with reason alone?

All life is a struggle in the dark.

As children in blank darkness tremble, afraid of everything, so we in broad daylight are oppressed at times by fears as baseless as those horrors which children imagine coming upon them in the dark. This dread and darkness of the mind cannot be dispelled by the sunbeams, the shining shafts of day, but only by an understanding of the visible form and inner workings of nature.

16 — New business: Birth, motion, and decay

Back to business. I will explain:

The motion by which the generative bodies of matter give birth to various things.

How things after they are born dissolve once more; the force that compels them to do this; and the power of movement through the boundless void with which they are endowed.

It is for you to heed my words.

Be sure that matter does not stick together in a solid mass. We see that everything grows less and seems to melt away with the lapse of time and withdraw its old age from our eyes. And yet we see no diminution in the sum of things. This is because the bodies that are shed lessen the thing they leave but enlarge the thing they join; here they bring decay, there full bloom, but they do not settle.

[Passing the torch] So the sum of things is perpetually renewed because mortals live by mutual interchange. Races wax and others wane. The generations of living things pass in swift succession, passing on the torch of life like runners in a race.

If you believe that the atoms can stop and by their stopping generate new motions in things, you are wandering far from the path of truth. Since the atoms are moving freely through the void, they must all be kept in motion either by their own weight or on occasion by the impact of another atom.[13] For it must often happen that two of them in their course knock together and immediately bounce apart in opposite directions, a natural consequence of their hardness and solidity and the absence of anything behind to stop them.

As further proof that all particles of matter are on the move, remember that the universe is bottomless: there is no place where the atoms could come to rest. As I have already shown by various arguments and proved conclusively, space is without end or limit, spreading out immeasurably in all directions alike.

It then follows that no rest is given to the atoms in their course through the depths of space. Driven along in an incessant but random motion, some of them bounce far apart after a collision while others recoil only a short distance from the impact. From those that do not recoil far, being driven into a closer union and held there by the entanglement of their interlocking shapes, are composed firmly rooted rock, the stubborn strength of steel and the like. Those others that move freely through larger tracts of space —few and far between, springing far apart and carried far by the rebound— these provide for us thin air and blazing sunlight.

Besides these, there are many other atoms at large in empty space that have been thrown out of compound bodies, and prohibited admittance so as to bring their motions into harmony.

An apt image —that is continually taking place before our very eyes— illustrates this process. **[Illustration from the motes in the sunbeam]** Observe what happens when sunbeams are admitted into a building and shed light on its shadowy places. You will see a multitude of tiny particles mingling in a multitude of ways in the empty space within the actual light of the beam, as if shoving in endless conflict, rushing into battle rank upon rank with never a moment's pause in a rapid sequence of unions and disunions. From this you may picture how atoms are perpetually tossed about in the infinite void.

To some extent a small thing may give an illustration and an imperfect image of great things. Besides, there is a further reason why you should study these particles that are seen dancing in a sunbeam: their dancing is an actual signal of the underlying motion of matter that is hidden from sight. There you will see many particles under the impact of invisible blows changing their course and driven back upon their tracks, this way and that—in all directions.

You must understand that they all get their restlessness from the atoms. It originates with the atoms, which move of themselves. Then those small compound bodies that are least removed from the impetus of the atoms are set in motion by the impact of their invisible hits and in turn explode against slightly larger blows. So the movement scales up from the atoms, gradually emerging to the level of our senses, so that those bodies are in motion that we see in sunbeams, moved by blows that remain invisible.

[Velocity of the atoms] As to the rate at which the atoms move, Memmius, you may gauge this from these few indications. First, when dawn sprays the earth with new-born light and the birds, flitting through pathless thickets, fill the area according to their kind with liquid notes that glide through the thin air, it is plain and palpable for all to see how fast the sun at the moment of his rising drenches and clothes the world with his radiance.

But the heat and the bright light that the sun spews do not travel through empty space. Therefore they are forced to move more slowly, cleaving their way as it were through waves of air. And the atoms that compose this radiance do not travel as isolated individuals but linked and massed together, so that their pace is retarded by one dragging back another as well as by external obstacles. But, when separate atoms are travelling in solitary solidity through empty space, they find no outside obstruction, moving as single units, being composed of their own parts, on the trajectory on which they have embarked.

Obviously then they must far outpace the sunlight in speed of movement and traverse an extent of space many times as great in the time it takes for the sun's rays to flash across the sky ...No wonder that men cannot follow the individual atoms, so as to discern the agency by which everything is brought about.

[False theory that the world is made for men by divine power] Even in the face of these truths, some people who know nothing of matter believe that nature without the guidance of the gods could not cause: the changing seasons in such perfect conformity to human needs; thus creating the crops and those other blessings that mortals are led to enjoy by the guide of life, divine pleasure, which coaxes them through the arts of Venus to reproduce their kind, lest the human race should perish.

Obviously, in believing that the gods establish everything for the sake of men, they stumble in all respects far from the path of truth.

Even if I knew nothing of the atoms, I would dare assert on the evidence of the celestial phenomena themselves, supported by many other arguments, that **the universe was certainly not created for us by divine power: it is so full of imperfections.**

All this, Memmius, I will make even more sense for you at a later stage. Now let me complete my account of atomic movements.

17 — The motion of the atoms

It is high time to insert a demonstration:

No *material thing can be uplifted or travel upwards by its own power.*

Do not be misled by the particles that compose flame. The fact that all weights taken by themselves fall downwards does not prevent lusty crops and trees from being born with an upward thrust and from growing and increasing upwards.

Likewise, when fires leap up to the housetops and lick beams and rafters with rapid flame, it must not be accepted that they do this of their own accord with no force to fling them up. Their behavior compares to that of blood released from our body when it spouts forth and springs aloft in a gory fountain. Also, observe with what force beams and rafters are heaved up by water. The more we have shoved them down into the depths, many of us struggling strenuously together to push them under, the more forcefully the water spews and ejects them back again, so that more than half their bulk shoots up above the surface.

Despite all this, I should judge, we have no doubt that all these, taken by themselves, would move downwards through empty space. It must be just the same with flames: under pressure they can shoot up through the gusty air, though their weight, taken by itself, strives to tug them down.

Don't we see how the nocturnal torches of the sky in their lofty flight draw in their wake long trails of flame in whatever direction nature has set their course?

Don't you see how stars and meteors fall upon the earth?

The sun from the summit of the sky scatters heat in every direction, sowing the fields with light. Therefore, the sun's radiance tends also towards the earth. Note again how the lightning flies through the rain-storms aslant. The fires that break out of the clouds rush together, now this way, now that, with the fiery force falling upon the earth often enough.

In this same point there is another fact that I want you to grasp:

When the atoms are traveling straight down through empty space by their own weight, at quite indeterminate times and places they swerve ever so little from their course.

But just so much that you can still call it a change of direction. Were it not for this swerve, everything would fall downwards like raindrops through the abyss of space. No collision would take place and no impact of atom upon atom would be created. Thus nature would never have created anything.

[False theory that heavier atoms fall faster than lighter]
If anyone believes that heavier atoms on a straight course through empty space could outpace lighter ones and fall on them from above, thus causing impacts that might give rise to generative motions, he is going far astray from the path of truth.

Objects falling through water or thin air must accelerate their fall in proportion to their weight simply because the matter composing water or air cannot obstruct all objects equally, but is forced to give way more speedily to heavier ones. But empty space can offer no resistance to any object in any region at any time, so as not to yield free passage as its own nature demands. Therefore, through undisturbed vacuum all bodies must travel at equal speed though impelled by unequal weights.

The heavier will never be able to fall on the lighter from above or generate of themselves impacts leading to that variety of motions out of which nature can produce things.

We are then led back to the conclusion that the atoms

swerve a little, but only by a minimum, or we shall be caught imagining slantwise movements, and the facts will prove us wrong. For we see plainly and indisputably that weights, when they come tumbling down, have no power of their own to move aslant, so far as meets the eye. But who can possibly perceive that they do not diverge in the very least from a vertical course?

18 — About determinism and free will

Again, if all motion is always interconnected, the new arising from the old in a determinate order —if the atoms never swerve so as to originate some new movement that will snap the bonds of fate, the perennial sequence of cause and effect— what is the source of the free will possessed by living things throughout the earth?

[It starts from the will and then passes through all the limbs] What, I repeat, is the source of that willpower snatched from the fates, whereby we follow the path along which we are severally led by pleasure, swerving from our course at no set time or place but at the bidding of our own hearts? There is no doubt that on these occasions the will of the individual originates the movements that trickle through his limbs.

Picture this: when the starting-gates are flung back, how the racehorses in the eagerness of their strength cannot break away as suddenly as their hearts desire. This is because the whole supply of matter must first be mobilized throughout every member of the body: only then, when it is assembled and arranged continuously, can it respond to the prompting of the heart. So you may see that the beginning of motion is generated by the heart; starting from the voluntary action of the mind. Then it is transmitted throughout the body and the limbs. Quite different is our experience when we are shoved along by a blow inflicted with force by someone else; in which case it is obvious that all the matter of our body is set going and pushed along against our will, till the will manages to check it through the limbs.

Do you see the difference?

[Motion under compulsion] Although many men are driven by an external force and often checked involuntarily to advance or to rush headlong, yet something in the human breast fights against this force, resisting it, forcing this supply of matter —at times— to take a new course through our limbs and joints. Or is checked in its course and brought once more to a halt.

Similarly, you must recognize in the atoms the same possibility: besides weight and impact there must be a third cause of movement —the source of this inborn power of ours— since we see that nothing can come out of nothing. The weight of an atom prevents its movements from being completely determined by the impact of other atoms. But the fact that the mind itself has no internal necessity to determine its every act, forcing it to suffer in helpless passivity; this is due to the slight swerve of the atoms at no determinate time or place.

19 — The supply of matter in the universe

The supply of matter in the universe was never more tightly packed than it is now, or more widely spaced out.

[Unchangeable] Nothing is ever added to it or subtracted from it.

The motion of atoms today is no different from what it was in bygone ages and always will be the same. The things that regularly come into being will always continue to come into being in the same manner, growing and flourishing so far as each is allowed by the laws of nature.

The sum of things cannot be changed by any force.

There is no place into which any kind of matter might flee out of the universe, or out of which some newly risen force could break into the universe, transforming the whole nature of things and reversing their movements.

In this connection there is one fact that cannot surprise us:

Although all the atoms are in motion, their whole body appears to stand totally still.

Motionless, indeed, except for such movements as particular objects may make with their own bodies, given that the atoms all lie far below the range of our senses.

[Analogies from experience] Since these atoms are themselves invisible, their movements must also elude our observation. It is true that even visible objects, when set at a distance, often disguise their movements. Often on a hillside fleecy sheep, when they eat their lush pasture, slowly creep onward, lured this way or that by grass that sparkles with fresh dew, while the full-fed lambs gaily frisk and butt. And yet, when we gaze from a distance, we see only a blur: a white patch stationary on the green hillside.

Take another example. Mighty legions, waging war games, are thronging the plain with their maneuvers, the dazzling sheen flashing to the sky, and all around the earth is ablaze with bronze. The sounds of mighty marching men's feet roar down below, as noise of shouting strikes upon the hills, reverberating to the celestial vault. Wheeling horsemen gallop hotfoot across the plain, till it quakes under the fury of their charge. And yet there is a vantage-ground high among the hills from which all these appear immobile: a blaze of light stationary upon the plain.

20 — About the shapes and forms of matter

And now let's explore a new theme:

The characteristics of the atoms of all substances, the extent to which they differ in shape and the rich multiplicity of their forms.

Though there are many things of the same shape, they are *by no means* all identical with one another. And no wonder. When the multitude of them, as I have shown, is such that it is without limit or total, one must not expect that they should all be identical in build and configuration.

[Cause of distinction] Take the race of men, the tribes of scaly fish that swim in silence, the lusty herds, the creatures of the wild, and the many feathered breeds, those that throng the vivifying watery places by river-banks and springs and lakes, and those that flock and flutter through pathless woodlands.

Take a representative of any of these diverse species and you will still find that it differs in form from others of its kind. Otherwise the young could not recognize their mother or the mother her young. But we see that this can happen, and that individuals of these species are mutually recognizable no less than human beings.

Let's look at a familiar example.

Outside some stately shrine of the gods incense is smoldering on the altar. Beside it a slaughtered calf falls to the ground, breathing out from its breast a hot stream of blood. But the bereaved dam, roaming through green glades, scans the ground for the twin-pitted imprint of familiar feet, her eyes roving this and that way in search of the missing young one. Pausing, she fills the leafy thickets with her plaints. Time and again she returns to the byre, sore at heart with yearning for her calf. Succulent osiers and herbage fresh with dew and her favorite streams flowing level with their banks; all these are powerless to console her and banish her new burden of distress.

The sight of other calves in the lush pastures is powerless to distract her mind or relieve it of distress. So obvious is it that she misses something distinctive and recognized.

Likewise, baby kids hail their own long-horned dams with quavering voices. Frisky lambs pick out their own mothers from the bleating flock. So, at nature's bidding, each usually runs to its own milk-swollen udder.

Among ears of corn, whatever the kind, you will not find one just like another; but each will be marked by some distinctive feature. The same goes for the various shells we see painting the bosom of the land where the sea with pliant ripples laps on the thirsty sands of its winding shore. Here we find then proof upon proof that in the stream of atoms likewise, since they exist by nature and are not handmade to a fixed pattern, but there are certain individual differences of shape flying about.

[Variety as cause] On this principle it is quite easy to explain why the fire of lightning is far more forceful than our fire which springs from earthly torches. You can say that the heavenly fire of the lightning is of finer texture, being composed of smaller atoms, passing through apertures impervious to this fire of ours, which springs from wood and is generated by a torch.

Again, light passes through horn, but rain is dashed back. Why, if not because the particles of light are smaller than those that form the life-giving drops of water?

We also see that wine flows through a strainer as fast as it is poured in; but sluggish oil loiters. This, no doubt, is either because oil consists of larger atoms, or because these are more hooked and interlaced and, therefore, cannot separate as rapidly, so as to trickle through the holes one by one.

[Difference of taste] Here is a further example. Honey and milk, when they are rolled in the mouth, leave an agreeable sensation to the tongue. But bitter wormwood and astringent centaury gag the mouth awry with their nauseating flavor. You may readily infer that substances that titillate the senses agreeably are composed of *smooth round* atoms. Those that seem bitter and harsh are more tightly compacted of hooked particles and accordingly tear their way into our senses, ripping our bodies by their inroads.

The same conflict between two types of structures applies to things that strike the senses as good or bad. You cannot suppose that the rasping sawing of a screeching saw is formed of elements as smooth as the notes a minstrel's nimble fingers draw from the lyre-strings, molding it to melody.

Neither can you suppose that atoms of the same shape are entering our nostrils when stinking corpses are roasting as when the stage is freshly sprinkled with saffron of Cilicia and a nearby altar exhales the perfumes of the Orient. You cannot attribute the same composition to sights that feast the eye with color and those that make it hurt and weep or that appear loathsome and repulsive by their sheer ugliness.

[Pleasure and pain are determined by the shape of the particles] Nothing that pleases the senses is ever without a certain smoothness of the constituent atoms.

On the other hand, what is painful and harsh is characterized by a certain roughness of matter. Besides these there are some things that though not properly regarded as smooth, yet are not jagged with barbed spikes. These are characterized instead by slightly jutting ridges such that prick the senses rather than hurt them; they include such things as wine-lees and piquant endive. Hot fire, again, and cold frost pierce the senses of our body with teeth of a different pattern, as we learn from the different way they affect our sense of touch.

[Touch the ultimate cause of all sensation] Touch and nothing but touch (by all that men call holy!) is the cause of all our bodily sensations, whether we feel something seeping in from outside or are hurt by something born in the body or pleasurably excited by something going out in the procreation act of Venus.[14] It is touch again that is felt when the atoms are jarred by a knock so that they randomly and upset the senses: strike any part of your own body with your hand, and you will experience this for yourself.

There must, therefore, be great differences in the shapes of the atoms to provoke these different sensations.

Once again: things that seem to us hard and stiff must be composed of deeply indented and hooked atoms and held firm by their interlacing branches. Foremost in this class stand diamonds, with their stubborn indifference to blows. Next are the stout flints and the strength of hard iron and bronze that stands firm with shrieking protest when the bolt is shot.

In contrast, liquids must owe their fluid consistency to component atoms that are small and round. For poppy-seed can be drawn off as easily as if it were water; the globules do not hold one another back, and when they are jolted they tend to roll downhill as water does. A third class is constituted by things that you may see dissipate instantaneously: smoke, clouds, and flames. If their atoms are not all smooth and round, yet they cannot be jagged and interlaced. They must be such as to prick the body and even to penetrate rocks yet not to stick together. You may readily grasp that substances prickly to the senses are made of atoms which are sharp-pointed but not entangled.

Let's not be surprised to find that some things are both bitter and fluid as, for instance, sea water. This, being fluid, consists of smooth round atoms. It causes pain because of the admixture of many rough atoms, but with no need for these to be held together by hooks. Evidently they are spherical as well as rough, so that they can roll round and yet hit the senses. It can be shown that Neptune's bitter brine results from a mix of rougher atoms with smooth ones. There is a way of separating the two ingredients and viewing them in isolation by filtering the sweet fluid through many layers of earth so that flowing out into a pit loses its tang. It leaves behind the atoms of unpalatable brine because owing to their roughness they are more apt to stick fast in the earth.

To the above demonstration I will link on another fact which will gain credence from this context:

The number of different forms of atoms is finite.

If this were not so, some of the atoms would have to be of infinite magnitude. Inside the narrow limits of any single particle, there can be only a limited range of forms. Let's assume that atoms consist of three minimum parts, or enlarge them by a few more. When by placing parts at top or bottom and transposing left and right you exhaust all the possible variations of the shape of the whole atom that can be produced by rearranging its parts, and are left with no means of varying its form further except by adding other parts. Thence it will follow, if you wish to vary its form still further, that the arrangement will demand still other parts in exactly the same way.

Variation in shape goes with increase in size.

Therefore, you cannot accept that the atoms are

distinguished by an infinity of forms, unless you compel some of them to be of enormous magnitude, which I have already proved to be demonstrably impossible.

If this wasn't so, the richest robes of the Orient, resplendent with the Meliboean purple of Thessalian murex, or the gilded breed of peacocks, bright with laughing luster, would pale before some new color in things. The fragrance of myrrh and the flavor of honey would fall into contempt. The death notes of the swan and the intricate melody of Phoebus' lyre would be silenced in like manner. For things would always be surpassed by something more excellent. And, as all good things might yield to better, so might bad to worse. One thing would always be surpassed by another more offensive to nose or ear or eye or palate.

Since this is not the case, but things are bound by a set limit at either extreme, you must agree to a corresponding limit to the different forms of matter. Similarly there is a limited range, from fire to the icy frosts of winter and back again. There are extremes of heat and cold, with the intermediate temperatures completing the series. They have been created, therefore, a limited distance apart, since the extremes are marked at either end with two points, one made intolerable with flames, the other by stiff frosts.

I will add another fact to the above demonstration, a fact which will gain credibility from this context:

The number of atoms of any one form is infinite.

Since the varieties of form are limited, the number of uniform atoms must be unlimited. Or the totality of matter would be finite, which I have disproved in my verses, showing that the universe is kept going by an infinite succession of atoms, with the chain of impacts from all directions remaining unbroken.

[Animals rare in one place are common in another] You may object that certain species of animals are relatively rare, so that nature seems less fertile in their case. But some other zone or regions in remote lands may abound in these, making good the deficiency. Let's note as the outstanding example among quadrupeds the snaky-handed elephants. Countless thousands of these must have gone to the making of that impenetrable ivory wall with which India is barricaded. Out of the abundance of these beasts we see only very few samples.

Let us suppose for argument's sake that one unique object exists, with a body formed by birth: an object like no other in the whole world.

Unless there is an infinite supply of matter from which, once conceived, it can be brought to birth, it will have no chance even of being created, nor prospect of further growth or renewal. Let us further assume that a finite number of atoms generative of one particular thing are at large in the universe. What then will be the source, scene, agency, or mode, of their encounter in this immeasurable ocean of matter, this mass of foreign bodies?

I see no possible way by which they could come together.

Imagine, when some great flotilla has been wrecked, how the mighty deep scatters the flotsam: thwarts and ribs, yard-arms and prow, masts and oars; how stern-posts are seen adrift off the shores of every land, a warning to mortals to shun the stealth and violence and cunning of the traitorous sea and put no faith at any time in the false alluring laughter of that smooth still surface. Just so will your finite class of atoms, if once you posit such a thing, be scattered and tossed about through all eternity by conflicting tides of matter. They could never be swept together so as to enter into combination, nor could they remain combined or grow by increment.

Yet experience clearly shows that both these things happen: objects are born, and after birth they grow. In conclusion: there are infinite atoms of every kind to keep up the supply of everything.

[Creation and destruction wage equal warfare] The destructive motions can never perpetually get the upper hand and entomb vitality for evermore. Neither can the generative and augmentative motions permanently protect what they have created. So the raging war of the elements that has gone throughout eternity goes on equal terms. Now here, now there, the forces of life are triumphant and in turn defeated. With the voice of mourning mingles the cry that infants raise when their eyes open on the sunlit world. Never has day given place to night or night to dawn that has not heard, blended with these infant wailings, the mourning that attends on death and somber obsequies.

In this respect there is one fact that you should keep signed and sealed and recorded in the archives of memory:

There is no visible object that consists of atoms of one kind only.

Everything is composed of a mixture of elements. The more qualities and powers a thing possesses, the greater variety it attests in the form of its component atoms.

[**Earth has every kind**] In the first place the earth contains in itself the atoms with which the vast ocean is perpetually renewed by streams that roll down coolness, containing also matter from which fires can arise: in many places the soil is set alight and burns, and subterranean fires sustain the furious outrush of Etna.

[**Mother Earth**] In addition, it contains the stores out of which it can thrust up thriving crops and lusty orchard-trees for the races of mankind, providing rivers and foliage and lush pasture for the wild beasts of the mountain. That is why this one being has earned such tides as Great Mother of the Gods, Mother of Beasts and mother of the human frame.

[**Goddess Earth**] This is she who was hymned by learned Greek poets of old. They pictured her as a goddess,[15] driving a chariot drawn by a yoke of lions, signifying that the whole mighty mass hangs in airy space: for earth cannot rest on earth. They harnessed wild beasts, because the fiercest of children cannot but be softened and subdued by the duty owed to parents. On her head they set a battlemented crown, because earth in select spots is fortified and bears the weight of cities.

Bedecked with this emblem even today the image of the

Holy Mother, Cybele, is borne about the world in solemn state. Various nations hail her with time-honored ceremony as the Idaean mother. To bear her company they appoint a Phrygian retinue, claiming that crops were first created within the bounds of Phrygia and spread from there throughout the earth. They give her eunuchs as attendant priests, to signify that those who have defied their mother's will and shown ingratitude to their parents must be judged unworthy to bring forth living children into the sunlit world. A thunder of drums attends her, tight-stretched and pounded by palms, and a clash of hollow cymbals; hoarse-throated horns bray deep warnings, the hollow pipe thrilling every heart with Phrygian strains. Knives are displayed before her, symbolic of wild frenzy, to punish the thankless and profane hearts of the rabble with dread of her divinity. So, when first she is escorted into some great city mutely enriching mortals with some wordless benediction, strewing her path all along the route with a lavish abundance of copper and silver and shadowing the mother and her retinue with a snow of roses. Next an armed band, whom the Greeks call *Curetes,* join in rhythmic dances, wild with blood, nodding their heads to set their terrifying crests aflutter, as they joust together among the Phrygian bands.

They remind us of those Curetes of Dicte, who long ago in Crete, as the story goes, drowned the wailing of the infant Jove by dancing with swift feet, an armed band of boys around a boy, and rhythmically clashing bronze on bronze, under threat that Saturn should seize and crush him in his jaws and deal his mother's heart a wound that would not heal.

That perhaps is why they attend in arms upon the Great Mother.

[Yet all this is false] Or else it means that the goddess commands men to be ready to forcefully defend their native earth with arms and resolve, shielding their parents, and giving them credit. It may be claimed that all this is aptly and admirably devised, yet it far removed from the truth.

[The gods live in a placid life apart from the world]

Aloof and detached from human affairs, the very nature of the deity requires that it should own and enjoy immortal existence in utter tranquility.

Free from all pain and peril —the deity— becomes strong in its own resources, exempt from any need of humans, impervious to our merits, and immune from anger.

In fact, the earth is and always has been an insentient being. The reason why it sends up countless things in countless ways into the sunlight is simply that it contains atoms of countless substances.

If a person[16] elects to call the sea Neptune and the crops Ceres and would rather take Bacchus' name in vain than denote grape juice by its proper title, we may allow this person to refer to the earth as the Mother of the Gods, as long as he genuinely refrains from polluting his mind with the foul stain of superstition.

Frequently we see that fleecy flocks and martial steeds and horned cattle eat the herbage of a single field under the same canopy of sky, quenching their thirst with the water of a single stream. Yet they live according to their own kind while severally keep the nature of their parents, copying their behavior. So varied is the store of matter in every sort of herb and in every stream.

In addition, every individual animal of any species is a whole made up of various parts: bones, blood, veins, heat, moisture, flesh, and sinews; but all these parts are widely different, being formed of differently shaped atoms.

[Different bodies contain the seeds of fire] Again, a thing whatever can be set on fire and burned must conceal in its body, if nothing else, at least the matter needed for emitting fire and radiating light, for shooting out sparks and scattering ashes all around. If you mentally examine anything else by a similar procedure, you will find that it hides in its body the seeds of many substances and combines atoms of various forms.

You see that many objects possess color and taste together

with smell. Principal among them are those many offerings which when kindled make the altars of the gods to smoke. Their component matter must therefore be multiform. Scent penetrates the human frame where tint does not go; tint gets into the senses by a different route from taste. From which you may infer that they differ in their atomic forms.

Hence, different shapes combine in a single mass, and objects are composed of a mixture of seeds.

In my verses, for instance, you see many letters common to many words; yet you must admit that different verses and words are composed of different letters. Not because there is any lack of letters common to several words, or that there are no two words composed of precisely the same letters; but because words do not all alike consist of exactly the same components. So in other things, although many atoms are common to many substances, yet these substances may still differ in their composition.

So we can rightly say that the human race differs in its composition from crops or orchard trees.

It must not be assumed that atoms of every sort can be linked in every variety of combination.

If that were the case, you'd see monsters coming into being everywhere. Hybrid growths of man and beast would arise, with lofty branches spreading here and there from a living body. Limbs of land-beast and sea-beast would often be conjoined. Chimeras breathing flame from hideous jaws would be spawned by nature throughout the all-generating earth.

But it is evident that nothing of this sort happens.

Everywhere we see that everything is created from specific seeds and born of a specific mother and grows up true to its type. We may infer that this is determined by some specific necessity. In every individual the atoms of its own kind, derived from all its food, disperse through its limbs and link together so as to set going the appropriate motions.

But we also see extraneous matter cast back by nature into the earth; and much is expelled from the body, under the impact of blows, in the form of invisible particles which could not link on anywhere or harmonize with the vital motions within so as to copy them.

Do not believe that these laws apply to animals alone. The same principle determines everything.

[Each thing has its appropriate seeds, food, and movements] As all created things differ from one another by their entire natures, so each one must of necessity consist of distinctive forms of atoms. Not that there is any lack of atoms of the same forms; but objects do not all alike consist of exactly the same components. Since the seeds are not identical, they must differ in their intervals, paths, attachments, weights, impacts, clashes and motions. These not only mark one animal body from another, but also separate land from sea and hold the whole sky apart from the earth.

21 — About colors

Lend ear now to arguments that I have searched out with an effort that was also a delight. Do not imagine that white objects derive the snowy aspect they present to your eyes from white atoms, or that black objects are composed of a black element. And in general do not believe that anything owes the color it displays to the fact that its atoms are tinted correspondingly.

The primary particles of matter have no color whatsoever, neither the same color as the objects they compose nor a different one.

If you think the mind cannot conceive of such bodies, you are quite wrong. Men born blind and having never looked on the sunlight have knowledge by touch of bodies that have never from the beginning been associated with any color. It follows that our minds also can form images of bodies not marked by any tint. In fact, the things that we ourselves touch in pitch darkness are not felt by us as possessing any color.

Having proved that colorless bodies are not unthinkable, I will proceed to prove that the atoms must be such bodies.

First, then, all colors may change completely, and all things that change color also change themselves. But the atoms cannot possibly change color: a thing must remain changeless, or everything would be absolutely annihilated.

If ever a thing is so transformed as to overstep its own limits, this means the immediate death of what was before. So do not stain the atoms with color, or you will find everything slipping back into nothing.

[The variety of atoms account for different colors] Let us assume then that the atoms are naturally colorless and that it is through the variety of their shapes that they produce the whole range of colors, with a great deal depending on their combinations and positions and their reciprocal motions. You will now find it easy to explain without wasting any time why things that were dark-colored a moment since can suddenly become as white as marble; as the sea, for instance, when its surface is ruffled by great winds, turning into white wave-crests of marble luster. You could say that something we often see as dark is promptly transformed through the churning up of its matter and a reshuffling of atoms, with some additions and subtractions, so that it is seen as bleached and white. If, on the other hand, the waters of the sea were composed of blue atoms, they could not possibly be whitened: for, however you may stir up blue matter, it can never change its color to the pallor of marble.

It might be supposed that the uniform sheen of the sea is made up of particles of different colors, as for instance a single object of a square shape is often made up of other objects of various shapes. But in the square, we discern the different shapes. So in the surface of the sea or in any other uniform luster we ought, on this hypothesis, to discern a variety of widely different colors. Besides, differences in the shapes of the parts are no hindrance to the whole being square in outline. But differences in color wholly prevent it from displaying a uniform luster.

The alluring argument that at times tempts us to assign colors to the atoms is demolished by the fact that white objects are not created from white material nor black from black, but both from various colors. It is obvious that white could much more readily spring from no color at all than from black, or from any other color that interferes and conflicts with it.

[Color needs light] Again, since there can be no colors without light and the atoms do not emerge into the light, it can be inferred that they are not clothed in any color. For what color can there be in blank darkness?

In truth, color is itself changed by a change of light, according as the beams strike it vertically or aslant.

Let's see in sunlight the colors of the plumage that rings the neck of a dove and crowns its nape: sometimes it is tinted with the brilliant red of a ruby: at others it is seen from a certain point of view to mingle emerald greens with the blue of the sky. Likewise, a peacock's tail, profusely illuminated, changes color as it is turned this or that way. These colors, then, are produced by a particular incidence of light.

Hence: no light—no color.

When the pupil of the eye is said to perceive the color white, it experiences in fact a particular kind of impact. When it perceives black, or some other color, the impact is different. But, when you touch things, it makes no difference what color they may be, but only what is their shape. The inference is that the atoms have no need of color, but cause various sensations of touch according to their various shapes.

Since there is no natural connection between particular colors and particular shapes, atoms might equally well be of any color irrespective of their form.

Why then aren't their compounds tinted with every shade of color irrespective of their kind? We should expect on this hypothesis that ravens in flight would often emit a snowy sheen from snowy wings: and that some swans would be black, being composed of black atoms, or would display some other uniform or be multi-colored.

Again, the more anything is divided into tiny parts, the more you can see its color gradually dimming and fading out. For example, when red cloth is pulled to pieces thread by thread, its crimson or scarlet of unmatched brilliance is all dissipated. From this you may gather that, before its particles are reduced right down to atoms, they would shed all their color.

[So atoms are without color, too] Finally, since you admit that not all objects emit noise or smell, you accept *that* as a reason for not attributing sounds and scents to everything. On the same principle, since we cannot perceive everything by eye, we may infer that some things are colorless, just as some things are scentless and soundless, and that these can be grasped by the percipient mind as readily as things that are lacking in some other quality.

22 — About other sensory qualities

Do not imagine that color is the only quality that is denied to the atoms.

They are also wholly devoid of warmth and cold and scorching heat: they are barren of sound and starved of savor, and emit no inherent odor from their bodies.

When you prepare a pleasant perfume of marjoram, myrrh, or flower of spikenard, which emits nectar into our nostrils, your first task is to select so far as possible an oil that is naturally colorless and sends out no exhalation to our nostrils, an oil least likely to corrupt and contaminate the scents blended with its own taint. In the same way the atoms must not emit to things at their birth a scent or sound that is their own property, since they can send nothing out of themselves; nor must they add any flavor or cold or heat, whether scorching or mild, or anything else of the kind.

Given that these qualities, again, are temporary and made pliable by the softness of their substance, breakable by its brittleness, and penetrable by its porousness of texture—they must be kept far apart from the atoms, if we wish to provide the universe with solid foundations on which it may rest secure; or else you will find everything slipping back into nothing.

23 — Of things sentient and insentient

At this stage you must admit that:

W*hatever is seen to be sentient is nevertheless composed of atoms that are insentient.*

The phenomena open to be examine do not contradict this conclusion or conflict with it. Rather they lead us by the hand, compelling us to believe that the animate is born, as I maintain, of the insentient.

As a particular example let's point to living worms, emerging from foul dung when the earth is soaked and rotted by intemperate showers.

Besides, we see every sort of substance transformed in the same way: rivers, foliage and lush pastures are transformed into cattle; the substance of cattle is transformed into our bodies, with enough of our bodies going to build up the strength of predatory beasts or the bodies of the lords of the air.

So does nature transform all foods into living bodies, generating from them all the senses of animate creatures; just as it makes dry wood blossom out in flame and transfigures it wholly into fire.

So it really makes a great difference in what order the various atoms are arranged and with what others they are combined so as to impart and take over motions.

What is it, then, that jogs the mind itself, moving and compelling it to express certain sentiments, so that you do *not* believe that the sentient is generated by the insentient?

Obviously, it is the fact that a mixture of water and wood and earth cannot of itself bring about vital sensibility. There is one relevant point you should bear in mind: I am not maintaining that sensations are created automatically from all the elements out of which sentient things are created. Each thing depends on the size and shape of the sense-producing atoms and on their appropriate motions, arrangements and locations. None of these is found in wood or clods of earth. And yet these substances, when they are fairly well decayed by showers, give birth to little worms, because the particles of matter are jolted out of their old arrangements by a new factor and combined in such a way that animate objects must result.

Those theorists who would have it that sensation can be produced *only* by sensitive bodies, which originate in their turn from others similarly sentient—these theorists risk to make the foundations of our senses perishable, because they are making them soft.

All this follows from the idea that sensitivity is always associated with flesh, sinews, veins: all things that we see to be soft and composed of perishable stuff.

Let us assume, for argument's sake, that particles of these substances could endure forever. The sensation with which they are credited must be either that of a part or else similar to that of an animate being as a whole. But it is impossible for parts by themselves to experience sensation: all the sensations felt in our limbs are felt by us as a whole; a hand or any other member severed from the whole body is quite powerless to retain sensation on its own.

But there remains the alternative that such particles have senses like those of an animate being as a whole.

They then must feel exactly what we feel, so as to share in all our vital sensations. How then can they pass for elements and escape the path of death, since they are animate beings, and animate and mortal are one and the same thing? Even if they could escape death, yet they will make nothing by their combination and union but a mob or horde of living things, just as men and cattle and wild beasts obviously could not combine so as to give birth to a single thing.

If we suppose that they shed their own sentience from their bodies and acquire another one, what is the point of giving them the one that is taken away? Besides, as we saw before, from the fact that we see birds' eggs turning into live fledglings and worms swarming out when the earth has been rotted by severe showers, we are justified to infer that sense may be created from the insentient.

[Sensation cannot arise from the insensate by change of

birth] Furthermore, suppose someone asserts that sense can indeed emerge from the insentient, but only by some transformation or some creative process equal to birth. He will be fairly answered by clearly demonstrating that birth and transformation occur only as the result of union or combination.

Admittedly, sensation cannot arise in anybody until an animate creature has been born.

This is because the requisite matter is dispersed through air and streams and earth and the products of earth: this matter has not yet come together in the appropriate manner, so as to set in mutual operation those vivifying motions that kindle the all-watchful senses which keep watch over every animate creature.

When any animate creature is unexpectedly assailed by a more powerful blow than its nature can withstand all the senses of body and mind are immediately thrown into confusion. For the juxtapositions of the atoms are unknotted, and the vital motions are inwardly obstructed, until the matter, jarred and jolted throughout every limb, loosens the vital knots of the spirit from the body, expelling the spirit in scattered particles through every pore.

[A blow puts an end to sensation because it dissolves unions and stops the vital motion] What other result can we attribute to the infliction of a blow than this of shaking and shattering everything to bits?

Besides, it often happens, when the blow is less violently inflicted, that such vital motions as survive emerge victorious, lessening the immense upheavals resulting from the shock, recalling every particle to its proper courses, and breaking up the advance of death. Thus it becomes master of the body that rekindles the well-nigh extinguished senses. How else could living creatures on the very throes of death rally their consciousness and return to life rather than make good their departure by a route on which they have already travelled most of the way?

[Pleasure and pain are caused by the internal

movements of atoms] Again, pain occurs when particles of matter have been disturbed by some force within the living flesh of the limbs and stagger in their inmost stations. When they are restored back into place—that is blissful pleasure! It follows that the atoms cannot be afflicted by any pain, or feel any pleasure in themselves, since they are not composed of any primal particles, by some reversal of whose movements they might suffer anguish or reap some fruition of life-giving bliss. They *cannot* therefore be endowed with any power of sensation.

[Reduction ad absurdum] Once again, if we are to account for the power of sensation possessed by animate creatures in general by attributing sentience to their atoms, what of those atoms that specifically compose the human race? Presumably they are not merely sentient, but also shake their sides with uproarious guffaws, besprinkling their cheeks with dewy teardrops; even discoursing profoundly and at length about the composition of the universe and proceed to ask of what elements they are themselves composed.

If they are to be equated to entire mortals, they must certainly consist of other elemental particles, and these again of others. There is no point at which you may call a halt, but I will follow you there with your argument that whatever speaks or laughs or thinks is composed of particles that do the same.

Let us acknowledge that this is stark insanity and lunacy.

One can laugh without being composed of laughing particles, and can think and proffer learned arguments though sprung from seeds neither thoughtful nor eloquent. Why then cannot the things that we see gifted with sensation be a composite of seeds that are wholly senseless?

[Earth is the universal mother] Finally, we are all sprung from heavenly seed. All alike have the same father, from whom all-nourishing mother earth receives the showering drops of moisture. Once fertilized, she gives birth to smiling crops and lusty trees, to mankind, and all the breeds of beasts. She yields the food on which they all feed their bodies, lead their joyous lives, renewing their race. So she has well-earned the name of mother.

Similarly, this matter returns: what came from earth goes back into the earth; what was sent down from the ethereal vault is readmitted to the precincts of heaven.

[Death is not destruction but reformation] Death does not put an end to things by annihilating the component particles but by breaking up their union. Next it links and recombines them, making everything change in shape and color and give up in an instant the gift of sensation it has just acquired. So you may realize what a difference it makes in what combinations and positions the same elements occur, and what motions they mutually pass on and take over.

You will in this manner avoid the mistake of conceiving as permanent properties of the atoms the qualities that are seen floating on the surface of things, coming into being from time to time and as suddenly perishing.

Obviously, it makes a great difference in my verses in what context and order the letters are arranged. For the letters which denote sky, sea, earth and rivers also denote crops, trees and animals. If not all, at least the greater part is alike. But differences in their order distinguish word from word. Just so with actual objects: to a change in the combination, motion, order, position or shapes of the component matter, there must be a corresponding change in the object composed.

24 — Other earths, other races of men

Give your mind now to the true reasoning I will unfold.

A new fact is struggling strenuously for access to your ears. A new aspect of the universe is striving to reveal itself. But no fact is so simple that it is not harder to believe than to doubt at the first presentation.

[Infinite atoms meeting in finite space will from time to time produce other worlds than ours] By the same token, there is nothing so mighty or so marvelous that the wonder it evokes does not tend to diminish in time. Take first the pure and undimmed sheen of the sky and all that it enshrines: the stars that roam across its surface, the moon and the surpassing splendor of the sunlight. If all these sights were this moment displayed to mortal view for the *first time* by a swift unforeseen revelation, what miracle could be said to be greater than this? What would men before the revelation have been less prone to conceive as possible? Nothing, surely.

So marvelous would have been that sight, a sight which no one *now* —you will admit— thinks worthy of an upward glance into the luminous regions of the sky. So has habit blunted the appetite of our eyes.

Desist, therefore, from thrusting out reasoning from your mind because of its disconcerting novelty. Weigh it, rather, with discerning judgment. Then, if it seems to you true, give in. If it is false, brace yourself to oppose it. For the mind wants to discover by reasoning what exists in the infinity of space that lies out there, beyond the gates of this world: that region into which the intellect longs to peer and into which the free projection of the mind does actually extend its flight.

Here, then, is my first point. In all directions alike, on this or that side, upward or downward through the universe, there is no end.

This I have shown, and in truth the fact proclaims itself aloud and the nature of space makes it crystal clear. Granted, then, that empty space extends without limit in every direction and that seeds innumerable in number are rushing on countless courses through an unfathomable universe under the impulse of perpetual motion:

It is in greatly unlikely that this earth and sky is the only one to have been created.

Consequently, that all those particles of matter outside are accomplishing nothing.

This follows from the fact that our world has been made by nature through the spontaneous and casual collision and the multifarious, accidental, random, and purposeless gathering and coalescence of atoms whose suddenly formed combinations could serve on each occasion as the starting-point of substantial fabrics: earth, sea, sky, and the races of living creatures.

On every ground, therefore, you must admit that there exist elsewhere other clusters of matter similar to this one which the ether clasps in ardent embrace.

When there is plenty of matter available, when space is available and no cause or circumstance impedes, then surely things must be formed and activated. You have a store of atoms that could not be counted out by the whole population of living creatures throughout history. You have the same natural force to congregate them in any place precisely as they have been congregated here.

You are bound therefore to accept that in other regions there are other earths and various tribes of men and breeds of beasts.

[Nothing in nature is unique] Let's add to this the fact that nothing in the universe is the only one of its kind, unique and solitary in its birth and growth; everything is a member of a species comprising many individuals. Turning your mind first to the animals, you will find the rule applies to the brutes that prowl the mountains, to the double-breed of men, the voiceless scaly fish and all the forms of flying things. So you must admit that sky, earth, sun, moon, sea and the rest are not solitary, but rather numberless.

A firmly established limit is fixed for their lives, and their bodies, as they are a product of birth, no less than that of any creature that flourishes here according to its kind.

Bear this well in mind, and you will immediately see that:

N*ature is free and, uncontrolled by proud masters and runs the universe by herself without the aid of gods.*

For who —by the sacred hearts of the gods who pass their unruffled lives, their placid eons, in calm and peace!— who can rule the sum total of the measureless? Who can hold in coercive hand the strong reins of the unfathomable? Who can spin all the firmaments alike and build with the fires of ether all the fruitful earths? Who can be in all places at all times, ready to darken the clear sky with clouds and rock it with a thunderclap, launching bolts that may often wreck his own temples, or retire and spend his fury letting fly at deserts with that missile which often misses the guilty, but slays the innocent and blameless?

After the natal season of the world, the birthday of sea and lands and the uprising of the sun, many atoms have been added from without, many seeds contributed on every side by bombardment from the universe at large. From these the sea and land could gather increase: the dome of heaven gains more room to lift its rafters high above the earth, so that the air could climb upwards. From every corner of the universe atoms are being chipped and circulated to each thing according to its own kind: water goes to water, earth swells with earthy matter; fire is forged by fires, ether by ether.

At length everything is brought to its utmost limit of growth by nature—perfect mother of it all.

[Bodies grow so long as they take in more than they give out] This is reached when what is poured into the veins of life is no more than what flows and drains away. Yet growing-time of everything must halt; nature checks the increase of her own strength. The things you see growing merrily in stature and climbing the stairs of maturity step by step are those things that gain more atoms than they lose.

Though the food is easily introduced into all their veins, they themselves are not so widely expanded as to shed much matter and squander more than their age absorbs as nourishment. It must, of course, be conceded that many particles ebb and drain away from things. But more particles must accumulate, until they have touched the topmost peak of growth.

[Decay: when bodies lose more than can take in] Thereafter the strength and vigor of maturity is gradually broken, and age slides down the path of decay; obviously the bulkier a thing is and the more expanded when it begins to wane, the more particles it sheds, giving them off from every surface. The food is not easily distributed through all its veins, or supplied in fair quantities to make good the copious effluences it exudes. It is only natural that a thing should perish when it is thinned out by the ebbing out of matter and succumbs to blows from without. The food supply is no longer adequate for its aged frame, while the deadly bombardment of particles from without never pauses in the work of dissolution.

In this way the gates of the great world also will be breached and collapse in crumbling ruin about us, since everything must be restored and renewed by food, and by food that is buttressed and sustained. And the process is doomed to failure, because the veins do not admit enough and nature does not supply all that is needed.

Already the life-force is broken. The earth, which generated every living species and once brought forth from its womb the bodies of huge beasts, has now scarcely strength to generate tiny creatures. I am assuming that the races of mortal beings were not let down into the fields from heaven by a golden cord, nor spawned from the sea or the rock-beating surf, but born of the same earth that now nurtures it.

This same earth —in her prime— spontaneously generated for mortals the smiling crops and lusty vines, sweet fruits and gladsome pastures, which now can scarcely be made to grow by our toil. Wearing down the oxen and wearing out the strength of farmers, we run down the ploughshare, finding ourselves barely supplied by the fields that grudge their fruits and multiply our toil. Already the ploughman of ripe years shakes his head sighing that his heavy labors have gone for nothing: and, when he compares the present with the past, he praises his father's luck.

In the same unhappy vein, the cultivator of old and wilted vines condemns the trend of the times and curses heaven, complaining that past generations, when men were old-fashioned and god fearing, supported life easily enough on their small farms, though one man's holding was then far less than now.

He does not realize that everything is gradually decaying and being cast onto the rocks, worn out by old age.

BOOK THREE — LIFE AND MIND

25 — A prayer

[**Praise of Epicurus**] You, who out of such black void were first to lift up so shining a light, revealing the hidden blessings of life, you are my leader, Oh glory of the Grecian race.[17] In your well-marked footprints now I plant my firm steps. With love alone I wish to imitate you, not from emulous ambition.

Shall the swallow compete in song with the swan, or the kid match its wobbly legs in a race with the strong-limbed steed? You are our father, famed discoverer of truth, and give me a father's guidance. From your pages, as bees in flowery glades sip every blossom, so do I crop all your golden sayings, golden indeed, and forever worthy of everlasting life.

Your reasoning, springing from that godlike mind, lifts up its voice to proclaim the nature of the universe, so that the terrors of the mind take flight letting the gates of the world roll apart, and I see the march of events throughout the whole of space: the majesty of the gods is revealed in those quiet chambers, never ever shaken by storms, or drenched by rain-clouds, or defaced by white drifts of snow which a harsh frost congeals.

A limpid ether roofs them, laughing with radiance lavishly diffused. All their wants are supplied by nature, and nothing at any time blights their peace of mind. But nowhere do I see the banks of Acheron, though the earth is no barrier to my beholding all that passes underfoot in the space beneath. Seized with divine delight and a shuddering awe I am, seeing that by your power nature stands unveiled and made manifest in every part.

26 — Mind

[**The true nature of the soul**] I have already shown what

the component bodies of everything are like: how they vary in shape: how they tear spontaneously through space, impelled by a perpetual motion: and how from these all objects can be created.

Clearly, the next step now is to discern in my verses the nature of mind and of spirit. In so doing I must throw out the fear of Acheron head over heels; that fear which blasts the life of man from its very foundations, sullying everything with the blackness of death and leaving no pleasure pure and unalloyed.

Some men often speak of sickness or of shameful life as more to be dreaded than the lowest pit of death, claiming to know that the mind consists of blood, or maybe wind, if that is how the whim takes them, and to stand in no need whatever of our reasoning. But all this talk is due more to the desire to show off than on actual proof, as you may infer from their conduct.

[A crisis reveals the old fear of death] Although these same men may be exiled from home, banished far from the sight of their fellows, soiled with the accusation of some filthy crime, a prey to every torment—they still cling to life. Wherever they come in their tribulation, they make timely sacrifices, slaughter black cattle and dispatch offerings to the dead. The heavier their afflictions, the more piously they turn their minds to superstition.

Look at a man in the midst of trouble and danger, and you will learn in his hour of misfortune what he really is when his true utterances are wrung from the depths of his heart.

The mask is torn off, and his real self remains.

[The cause of vices and crime] Consider too the greed and blind lust of status that drive pathetic men to abused the bounds of right, even making them into accomplices or instruments of crime, striving night and day with unstinted effort to scale the pinnacles of wealth. These running sores of life are fed in no small measure by the fear of death: abject ignominy and annoying poverty seem far indeed from the joy and assurance of life, loitering already at the gateway of death. From such a fate men, in groundless terror, long to escape far far away. So in their greed of lucre they amass a fortune out of civil bloodshed, piling wealth on wealth they heap carnage on carnage.

With heartless glee they welcome a brother's tragic death, hating and fearing the hospitable board of their own kin. Often, in the same spirit and because of the same fear, they are consumed with envy at the sight of another's success: he walks in a blaze of glory, looked up to by all, while they curse the somber squalor in which their own lives are bogged.

Some sacrifice life itself for the sake of statues and a title.

From fear of death mortals are often gripped by such a hate of living and looking on the light that with anguished hearts they do themselves to death, forgetting that this fear is the very fountain-head of their troubles. This it is that harasses conscience, snaps the bonds of friendship and in a word totally destroys all moral responsibility.

Repeatedly, before now, men have betrayed their country and their beloved parents in an effort to escape the banks of Acheron.

[Science dispels darkness] As children in total darkness tremble and cower at everything, so we in broad daylight are oppressed at times by fears as groundless as those horrors which children imagine coming upon them in the dark. This dread and darkness of the mind cannot be ousted by the sunbeams, the shining shafts of day, but only by an understanding of the outward form and inner workings of nature.

[The mind is part of the body] First, I maintain that <u>the mind</u> which we often call the intellect, the seat of the guidance and control of life, *is a component of a man,* no less than hand or foot or eyes are parts of a whole living creature. Some who argue that the sentience of the mind doesn't reside in any particular part, but is a vital condition of the body, what the Greeks call a *harmony* which makes us live as sentient beings without having any locally determined mind. Just as good health may be said to belong to the healthy body without being any specific part of it; therefore, they do not station the sentience of the mind in any specific part.

In this they seem to be far off the mark.

Often enough the visible body is obviously ill, while in some other unseen part we are enjoying ourselves. No less often the reverse happens: one who is sick at heart enjoys bodily well-being. This is no different from the experience of an invalid whose foot is hurting while his head is in no pain.

Or consider what happens when we surrender our limbs to soothing slumber and our body, replete and relaxed, lies insensible. At that very time there is something else in us that is awake to all sorts of stimuli, something that gives free admittance to all the motions of joy and to heartaches void of substance.

[**No harmony**] Next, you must understand that *there is also a vital spirit in our limbs* and the body does not derive its sentience from any 'harmony.' In the first place, life often lingers in our limbs after a large part of the body has been cut off. On the other hand, when a few particles of heat have dispersed and some air has been let out through the mouth, next life abandons the veins and abandons the bones. Hence you may infer that all the elements do not hold equal portions of vitality or support it equally, but it is chiefly thanks to the atoms of wind and heat that life lingers in the limbs. Consequently, there is in the body itself a vital breath and heat which forsakes our limbs at death.

Now that we have discovered the nature of the mind and of the vital spirit as a part of the man, drop this name 'harmony' which was passed down to the musicians from the heights of Helicon, or else perhaps they fetched it themselves from some other source and applied it to the matter of their art, which had then no name of its own. Be that as it may, let them keep it. And give your attention now to the rest of my discourse.

27 — Spirit

Next, I maintain that *mind and spirit are interconnected,*

making between them one single substance.

But what I may call the head and the dominant force in the whole body is that guiding principle which we term mind or intellect. This is firmly lodged in the mid-region of the breast; here is the place where fear and alarm pulsate. Here is felt the caressing touch of joy. Here, then, is the seat of intellect and mind. The rest of the vital spirit, diffused throughout the body, obeys the mind and moves under its direction and impulse. The mind by itself experiences thought and joy of its own even at a time when nothing moves either the body or the spirit.

When our head or eye suffers from an attack of migraine, our whole body does not share in its aching. Just so the mind sometimes suffers by itself or jumps for joy when the rest of the spirit, diffused through every limb and member, remains unstirred by any new impulse. But, when the mind is upset by some more overwhelming fear, we see all the spirit in every limb upset in sympathy: sweat and pallor break out all over the body; speech grows inarticulate; the voice fails; the eyes grow dim; the ears buzz; the limbs totter.

Often we see men actually drop down because of the terror that has gripped their minds. Hence you may readily infer a link between the mind and the spirit, which, when shaken by the impact of the mind, immediately jostles and propels the body.

The same reasoning proves that *mind and soul are both composed of matter.*

We see both of them propelling the limbs, rousing the body from sleep, changing the expression of the face and guiding and steering the whole man with activities that all clearly involve touch, as touch in turn involves matter.

How then can we deny their material nature?

You see the mind sharing in the body's experiences and sympathizing with it. When the nerve-racking impact of a spear lays bare bones and sinews, even if it does not penetrate to the seat of life, there follows faintness and a soothing falling towards the ground and on the ground turmoil in the mind with an intermittent faltering impulse to stand up again.

The substance of the mind must therefore be material, since it suffers the impact of material weapons.

28 — Mind and its matter

My next task will be to demonstrate to you the sort of matter mind is composed of and how it was formed.

First:

It is very finely textured and composed of exceptionally minute particles.

Mark my words: you will be able to infer this from the following facts. It is evident that nothing happens as speedy as the mind represents and sketches the happening to itself. Hence, the mind sets itself in motion more swiftly than any of those things whose substance is visible to our eyes. But what is so mobile must consist of superbly spherical and tiny atoms, so that it can be set going by a slight push.

The reason why water is set going and flowing by such a slight push is of course not only the smallness of its atoms, but also by their readiness to roll. The stickier consistency of honey, its relatively sluggish flow, and slow progress is due to the closer coherence of the component matter, consisting, as it obviously does, of particles not so smooth or so fine or so round.

A high pile of poppy seed can be disturbed by a light puff of breeze, so that seed trickles down from the top, yet the breeze cannot do the same to a heap of stones or corn ears. Relatively, then, smaller and smoother objects enjoy more mobility, while the greater their weight and roughness, the more firmly are they anchored.

[Mind and soul are formed of very minute particles] Since, the substance of the mind has been found to be extraordinarily mobile, it must consist of particles superbly small, smooth, and round. This discovery, my good friend, will prove a timely aid to you in many problems.

Here is a further indication how delicate is the texture of

the vital spirit and in how small a space it could be contained if it could be massed together: at the instant when a man is overwhelmed and forsaken by mind and spirit by the carefree calm of death, you cannot tell either by sight or by weight that any part of the whole has been snatched from his body. Death leaves everything there, except vital sentience and warmth. Therefore the vital spirit as a whole must consist of very tiny atoms, linked together throughout veins, flesh, and sinews: atoms so small that, when all the spirit has escaped from the whole body, the outermost contour of the limbs appears intact and with no loss of weight.

A similar thing happens when the bouquet has evaporated from the juice of Bacchus, or the sweet aroma of an ointment has escaped into the air, or some substance has lost its savor. The substance itself is not visibly diminished by the loss, and its weight is not lessened, obviously because savor and scent are caused by many tiny atoms distributed throughout the mass.

Therefore, it may be inferred that *mind* and *spirit* are composed of exceptionally diminutive atoms, since their departure is not accompanied by any loss of weight.

Also, it must not be assumed that the stuff of mind or spirit is a single element.

At death the body a thin breath abandons the dying; breath that is mixed with heat, while the warmth carries with it also air, since heat never occurs without air being mixed with it. This is so because it is naturally sparse; it must then have many atoms of air moving in its interstices.

29 — A 'fourth element' rules the spirit

The composition of mind is thus so far found to be at least threefold.

[The fourth nature] But all these three components together are not enough to create sentience, since the mind does not admit that any of these can create the sensory motions that generate the thoughts of the mind. *We must* accordingly *add to these a fourth component,* which is quite nameless. Nothing is there more mobile or more tenuous than it; nothing whose component atoms are smaller or smoother. This is what first sets the sensory motions flowing through the limbs.

Owing to the minuteness of its atoms, it is first to be stirred.

Then the motions are caught up by warmth and the unseen energy of wind, then by air. Then everything is agitated to movement: the blood is quickened; the impulse spreads throughout the flesh; last of all, bones and marrow are thrilled with pleasure or the opposite excitement. To this extremity pain cannot lightly penetrate, or the pangs of anguish win through. If they do, then everything is so confounded that no room is left for life, or the parts of the vital spirit will escape through all the pores of the body.

A stop, though, is put to these movements as near as may be at the surface of the body; and that is how we contrive to cling on to life.

[Combination of elements] Now I should like to demonstrate *how these combinations are intermixed* and from what mode of combination they derive their powers. Reluctantly, I am frustrated in my task by the poverty of our native tongue. But, so far as I can touch upon the surface of this topic, I will take it on.

The atoms rush in and out among one another on atomic trajectories, so that no one of them can be segregated nor its distinctive power isolated by intervening space. They coexist like the many properties of a single body. In the flesh of any living thing there are regularly scent and color and taste; and yet from all these there is formed only one solid bulk. Just so, warmth and air and the unseen energy of wind create in combination a single substance, together with that mobile force which imparts to them from itself the initial impetus from which the sensory motion takes its rise throughout the flesh.

This basic substance lurks at our very core.

[The hidden fourth nature] Nothing in our bodies is more basic than this, the most vital element of the whole vital spirit.

Just as in our limbs and body as a whole mind and spirit with their interconnected powers are latent, because their component atoms are small and sparse, so this nameless element composed of minute atoms is latent in the vital spirit and is in turn its vital element that rules the whole body.

In the same way, wind and air and heat commingled through the limbs interact, one being relatively latent, another prominent. In appearance a single stuff is formed by them all: warmth and wind and air do not display their powers individually so as to blot out sentience and dissolve it by their disunion.

First, there is heat at the mind's disposal, which brings into play when it boils with rage and passion, blazing more fiercely from the eyes. Likewise, there is no lack of that chill wind, mate of fright, which makes the limbs tremble, impelling them to flight. There is lastly that calm and steady air which remains steadfast and tranquil in the breast, and unruffled in demeanor.

[Heat causes anger] A surplus of this hot element we find in those creatures whose passionate hearts and angry dispositions easily boil up in anger. An outstanding example is the aggressive temper of lions, who often roar till they burst their chests with bellowing, unable to keep the torrents of their rage held within their breasts. But the cold hearts of deer are of a windier blend: they are quicker to set chill breezes blowing through the flesh, causing a shuddering movement in the limbs. Cattle, again, have in their vital composition a bigger portion of calm air. They are never too hotly fired by a touch of that smoky torch of anger which clouds the mind with its black and blinding shadow. Never are they transfixed and benumbed by the icy shaft of fear; their nature is a mean between the timidity of the deer and the lion's ferocity.

So it is with men.

Though education may add a similar polish to various individuals, it still leaves deep traces of their several temperaments. Let's not assume that innate vices can be totally eradicated: one man will still incline too readily to outbursts of rage; another will give way to fear rather quicker; a third will accept some contingencies too passively. And in a host of other ways men must differ one from another in temperament, which affects their resultant behavior.

To treat here the secret causes of these differences is beyond my power.

I cannot even find names for the abundance of atomic shapes that give rise to this variety of types. But I am clear that there is one relevant fact I can affirm: the lingering traces of inborn temper that cannot be eliminated by philosophy are so slight that there is nothing to prevent men leading a life worthy of the gods.

This *vital spirit,* then, *is present in the whole body.*

[Union of soul and body is the cause of life] It is the body's guardian and preserver. The two are intertwined by common roots and cannot be torn apart without manifest disaster. As easily could the scent be torn out of lumps of incense without destroying their nature, as mind and spirit could be abstracted from the whole body without total dissolution. So from their earliest origin the two are charged with a communal life by the interlocked atoms that compose them. It is clear that neither body nor mind by itself without the other's aid possesses the power of sensation:

It is by the interacting motions of the two combined that the flame of sentience is kindled in our flesh.

Again, body by itself never experiences birth or growth, and we see that it does not persist after death. Water, we know, often gives up the heat imparted to it without being torn apart in the process and survives intact. The derelict's limbs cannot outlast the departure of the vital spirit: they are utterly demolished by internal decomposition and decay.

[Each needs the other] So from the very beginning, even when they are at rest in the mother's womb, body and spirit in mutual contact acquire the motions that generate life. They cannot be wrenched apart without hurt and havoc. Therefore, since their very existence depends upon conjunction, that their nature must likewise be conjoint.

[The body itself feels owing to its combination with soul] If anyone still *denies* that the body is sentient, and believes it is the spirit interfused throughout the body that assumes this motion which we term sensation, he is fighting against manifest facts. Who can explain what bodily sensation really is without confirming that it is palpably presented to us by experience? Granted, when the spirit is banished, the body is quite insensible. That is because what it loses was never one of its permanent properties, but one of many attributes which it loses at death.

[The eyes themselves see and are not 'doors to the soul.'] Again, it is impossible to maintain that the eyes can see nothing, but the mind peeps out through them as though through open doors. The sense of sight itself leads us the other way, dragging and tugging us right to the eyeballs; often, for instance, we cannot see bright objects, because our eyes are blinded by light. This is an experience unknown to doors: the doorways through which we gaze suffer no distress by being flung open. Besides, if our eyes are equivalent to doors, then when the eyes are removed the mind clearly should to see things better now that the doors are away, doorposts and all.

Another mistake that should be avoided and one that is allowed by the revered authority of the great Democritus: that the limbs are knit together by atoms of body and mind arranged alternately, first one and then the other. In fact, *the atoms of spirit are not only much smaller than those composing our body and flesh; they are also correspondingly fewer in number* and scattered but sparsely through our limbs. To be safe, you could say this: observe what are the smallest objects whose impact serves to excite sensory motions in our bodies — these will give you the measure of the gaps between the atoms of spirit. Sometimes we don't notice that dust is sticking to our bodies or a cloud of chalk has settled on our limbs, nor do we feel the night mist, or the slight threads of gossamer in our path that enmesh us as we walk. Or feel the fall of a flimsy cobweb on our heads, or feathers of birds or flying thistledown, which from their very lightness do not lightly descend.

We do not mark the path of every creeping creature that crawls across our body or all the separate footfalls planted by gnats and other creatures. So a considerable commotion must be made in our bodies before the atomic disturbance is felt by the atoms of spirit. Being interlaced through our limbs they must be disturbed before they can knock together across the intervening gaps, clashing and combining to once again bounce apart.

[The mind is more essential for life than the soul] Also, note that *it is mind, far more than spirit that keeps life under lock and key.* Mind has the greater mastery over life; without mind and intellect no scrap of vital spirit can linger one instant in our limbs.

Spirit follows smoothly in the wake of mind and scatters into the air, leaving the limbs cold with the chill of death.

While mind remains, life remains.

A person whose limbs are all lopped from the mangled trunk, despite the loss of vital spirit released from the limbs, yet lives and inhales the life-giving gusts of air. Though robbed, if not of all, at least of a large proportion of his spirit, he lingers still in life, clinging fast to it. Just so, though the eye is lacerated all round, so long as the pupil remains intact, the faculty of vision remains active, as long as you do not hack away the whole encircling orb and leave the eyeball detached and isolated; for that cannot be done without total destruction. But once that tiny bit in the middle of the eye is eaten away, then the light goes out there and then and darkness falls, despite the shining orb being otherwise unscathed. It is on just such terms that spirit and mind are everlastingly linked together.

30 — Minds and spirits: no birth no death

My next point is this: you must understand that the *minds of living things and the light fabric of their spirits are neither birthless nor deathless*. For this purpose I have long been garnering and inventing verses with a labor that is also a joy. Now I will try to set them out in a style worthy of your calling and character.

Please note that both objects are to be embraced under one name. When, for instance, I proceed to demonstrate that 'spirit' is mortal, you must understand that this applies equally to 'mind', since the two are so conjoined as to constitute a single substance.

First of all, then, I have shown that spirit is flimsy stuff composed of tiny particles. Its atoms are obviously far smaller than those of swift-flowing water or mist or smoke, since it far outpaces them in mobility, moving with a far impetus. Indeed, it is actually moved by images of smoke and mist. So, for instance, when we are in deep sleep, we may see altars sending up clouds of steam and giving off smoke; and we cannot doubt that we are here dealing with images. Now we see that water flows out in all directions from broken vessels, the fluid departing, and mist and smoke vanishing into thin air.

Spirit is similarly dispelled and vanishes far more speedily and is sooner dissolved into its component atoms once it has been let loose from the human frame. When the body, which served as a vessel for it, is by some means broken and diminished by loss of blood from the veins, so as to be no longer able to contain it, how can you suppose that it can be contained by any kind of air, which is a far less solid container than our bodily frame?

[Mind is born, grows, and ages with body] Now, we are conscious that both *mind* and *body* are born together, growing up and growing old together. With the weak and delicate frame of wavering childhood goes a like infirmity of judgment. The robust strength of ripening years is accompanied by a steadier resolve and a more mature strength of mind. Later, when the body is palsied by the potent forces of age and the limbs have collapsed with blunted vigor, the understanding falters, the tongue rambles and the mind totters: everything weakens and gives way at the same time. It is natural that the vital spirit should all evaporate like smoke, soaring into the gusty air, since we have seen that it shares the body's birth and growth and simultaneously wears out with the weariness of age.

[Mind and body both have pains] In addition, as the body suffers the horrors of disease and the pangs of pain, so we see the mind pierced with anguish, grief, and fear. What more natural than that it should likewise have a share in death?

Often enough in the body's illness the mind wanders.

It raves and babbles distractedly, at times drifting on a tide of drowsiness, with drooping eyelids and nodding head, into a deep and unbroken sleep, from which it cannot hear the voices or recognize the faces of those who stand around with streaming eyes and tear-stained cheeks, striving to recall it to life.

Since the mind is thus invaded by the contagion of disease, you must acknowledge that it is destructible: pain and sickness are the architects of death, as we have been taught by the fate of many men before us.

[Intoxication affects body and mind alike] Again, when the pervasive power of wine has entered into a man and its glow is dispersed through his veins, his limbs are weighed with heaviness; his legs stagger and stumble; his speech is slurred, his mind besotted; his eyes swim; there is a crescendo of shouts, hiccups, blustering; and all the other symptoms follow in due order. Why should this be, if not because the wanton wildness of the wine has power to upset the vital spirit within the body? And, since things can be dislodged and upset, this shows that the inroad of a slightly more potent attack would make an end of them and rob them of a future.

[Epilepsy and the soul] Or it may happen that a man is seized with a sudden attack of epilepsy before our eyes, falling as though struck by lightning, foaming at the mouth. Groaning, he trembles in every joint. He raves. Contracting his muscles, he writhes, gasping convulsively. He tires his limbs with tossing. The cause of the foaming is that the spirit, torn apart by the violence of the disease throughout the limbs, riots and whips up spray, just as the wild wind's fury froths the salt sea waves. The groans issuing from him are because his limbs are racked with pain and in general because atoms of vocal sound are expelled and whirled out in a lump through the mouth — their usual outlet, where the way is already paved for them. The raving occurs because mind and spirit are dislocated and, as I have explained, split up and scattered topsy-turvy by the same poison. Then, when the cause of the disease has passed its climax and the morbid secretion of the ill body has returned to its secret abode, then the man rises, swaying wobbly at first, returning bit by bit to all his senses and recovering his vital spirit. When mind and spirit in the body itself are a prey to such violent seizures and suffer such distressing dispersal, how can you think them capable of surviving apart from the body in the open air with the wild winds for company?

[Medicine can cure mind and body] Conversely, we see that the mind —like a sick body— can be cured and directed by medicine. This too is a premonition that its life is mortal. When you try to alter the mind or to direct any other natural object, it is fair to suppose that you are adding certain parts or transposing them or subtracting some trifle at any rate from their sum. But an immortal object will not let its parts be rearranged or added to, or the least bit drop off. For, if ever anything is so transformed as to transgress its own limits, causing the immediate death of what was before.

Being susceptible both to sickness (as I have shown) and to medicine, the mind shows the marks of mortality. So false reasoning is plainly confronted by true fact; every loophole is barred to its exponent, and by the two horns of a dilemma he is convicted of falsehood.

Again, we often see a man pass away little by little, losing all sensation of life limb by limb: first the toes and toenails lose their color; then the feet and legs die; after that the imprint of icy death steals by slow degrees through the other members. Since the vital spirit is thus dispersed and does not escape all at once in its entirety, it must be regarded as mortal. You may be tempted to suppose that it can shrink into itself through the body and draw its parts together and so withdraw sensibility from every limb. If that was the case, the place in which such a mass of spirit was concentrated ought to display a great degree of sensibility. Since there is no such place, it is evidently scattered forth torn into pieces, as I said before. In other words, it perishes. Let us, however, concede this false hypothesis and suppose that the spirit concentrates within the body of those who leave the light of day through a creeping palsy.

You must still acknowledge that spirit is mortal.

It makes no difference whether it is scattered to the winds and disintegrated, or concentrated and deadened. In either case, the victim as a whole is more and more drained of sensibility in every part, in which less and less of life remains.

[The mind like any other organ of sense, cannot exist without the body] The mind, again, is one part of a man, staying fixed in a particular spot, no less than the ears and eyes and other senses by which life is guided. Of course, our hand or eye or nostrils in isolation from us cannot experience sensation or even exist; in a very short time they rot away. Hence, mind cannot exist apart from body and from the man himself who is like a vessel for it — or if you choose you may picture it as something still more intimately linked, since body clings to mind by close ties.

Once again, mind and body as a living force draw their vigor and their vitality from their union. Without body, the mind alone cannot perform the vital motions. Bereft of vital spirit, the body cannot persist and exercise its senses. As the eye uprooted and separated from the body cannot see, so we perceive that spirit and mind by themselves are powerless.

It is only because their atoms are held in by the whole body, intertwined through veins and flesh, sinews and bones, and are not free to bounce far apart, that they are kept together so as to perform the motions that generate sentience. After death, when they are expelled out of the body into the gusty air, they cannot perform the sensory motions because they are no longer held together in the same way. The air indeed will itself be a body, and an animate one at that, if it allows the vital spirit to hang together and keep up those motions which it used to go through before in the sinews and the body itself. Here we have proof upon proof. You must perforce admit that, when the whole bodily shell crumbles after the expulsion of the vital breath, the senses of the mind and the spirit likewise crumble, since body and mind can only exist when joined together.

[The decay of the body testifies to the breaking up of the soul before departure] Again, the body cannot suffer the escape of the vital spirit without rotting away in a foul stench. How can you doubt, then, but that the spirit diffused in the depths of the body has come to the surface and evaporated like smoke? That explains why the body is transformed and collapses so utterly into decay: its inmost foundations are sapped by the effusion of the spirit through the limbs and through all the body's twisting channels and chinks. So there are many indications that the vital spirit escapes through the limbs torn into pieces and is already split up within the body before it slips out and glides into the gusty air.

Even while the vital spirit still lingers within the boundaries of life, it often seems, when something has violently upset it, as though it were fighting to escape and be wholly released from the body, as though the features were relaxing into deathbed stillness and every limb were ready to hang limp upon the bloodless trunk. It is at such times that we say 'the mind has failed' or 'he has lost consciousness.'

There is general alarm, and everyone is straining to hold fast onto life's last mooring. Then the mind and all the vital spirit are all churned up and both these, together with the body, are on the point of collapse, so that a slightly intensified force might shatter them. How can you doubt, then, that the fragile spirit once stripped of its shell and thrust out of the body into the open would be powerless not only to survive throughout eternity but even to persist for a single instant?

[No dying man feels his soul depart all at once] Not a

single person on the point of death seems to feel his spirit retiring intact right out of his body or rising first to his gullet and up through his throat. On the contrary, he feels that it is failing in a particular region which it occupies, just as he is conscious that his other senses are being extinguished each in its own sphere.

If our mind were indeed immortal, it would not complain of extinction in the hour of death, but would rather feel that it was escaping from confinement and sloughing off its garment like a snake.

Let's ask: why is mind or thought never born in head or feet or hands?

Why does it cling fast in every man to one spot or a specified region?

It can only be that a specific place is assigned to each thing where it can be born and survive. So every creature is created with a great diversity of members, whose mutual position is never reversed. One thing must duly follow another: flame is not born in a flood, nor frost begotten in fire.

[An immortal soul must have senses of its own]
Moreover, if the spirit is by nature immortal and can remain sentient when divorced from our body, we must credit it, I presume, with the possession of five senses. In no other way can we picture to ourselves departed spirits wandering through the Infernal Regions. So it is that painters and bygone generations of writers have portrayed spirits in possession of their senses. But eyes or nostrils or hand or tongue or ears cannot be attached to a bodiless spirit. Such a spirit cannot therefore be sentient or even less exist.

We feel that the sensation of living resides in the whole body and we see that the whole body is animate. Assume, then, that it is suddenly sliced through the middle by some swiftly delivered slash, so as to fall into two quite separate parts. Without doubt the vital spirit will also be severed and split in two along with the body. But what is cleft and falls apart obviously gives up all pretensions to be immortal.

[The soul survives in severed from the body temporarily] They say that in the heat and indiscriminate carnage of battle limbs are often lopped off by scythe-armed chariots so suddenly that the fallen member severed from the body lies writhing on the ground. Yet the mind and consciousness of the man cannot yet feel the pain: so abrupt is the hurt, and so intent the mind upon the business of battle. With what is left of his body he presses on with battle and bloodshed and does not grasp, it may be, that his left arm together with its shield has been lost, whirled away among the chargers by the chariot wheels with their predatory blades. Another doesn't realize that his right arm has gone, while he keeps struggling to climb aboard the chariot. Yet another, who has lost a leg, does his best to stand up, while on the ground at his side the dying foot twitches its toes. A head severed from the still warm and living trunk retains on the ground its lively features and open eyes till it has yielded up the last shred of spirit.

[Analogy of the snake] Or take for example a snake with flickering tongue, menacing tail and long body. Should you choose to hack both ends of it in many pieces with a blade, you will see, while the wound is still fresh, every several portion separately squirming and spattering the ground with gore, and the main part twisting back with its mouth to bite itself in the fierce agony of the wound.

Shall we say that in each of these parts there is an entire spirit?

On that hypothesis, however, it would follow that one animate creature had in its body many spirits. Actually, a spirit that was one has been split up along with the body. So, both alike must be reckoned mortal, since both alike are split into many parts.

[If the soul is eternal, we ought to remember a previous existence] Next, if the spirit is by nature immortal and is slipped into the body at birth, why do we retain no memory of an earlier existence, no traces left by antecedent events? If the mind's operation is so greatly changed that all record of former actions has been expunged, it is no long journey, in my judgment, from this experience to annihilation. So you must admit that the pre-existent spirit has died and the one that is now is a new creation.

Let us assume, for argument's sake, that the vital force of mind is introduced into us when the body is already fully formed, at the moment when we are born and step across the threshold of life. This theory does not square with the observed fact that the mind grows with the bodily frame and in the very blood. It would imply that the mind lived in solitary confinement, alone in its cell, and yet at the same time the whole body was overflowing with sensation.

Here then is proof upon proof that spirits are not to be regarded as birthless, nor yet as exempt from the law of death.

[If the soul entered they body from without, it could not be so closely connected with it] If they —spirits— were injected into our bodies from outside, it cannot be supposed that the two would be so intimately interlocked as they are shown to be by the clearest evidence. For spirit so permeate veins, flesh, sinews, bones, that our very teeth share in sensation; to wit, toothache and the twinge of icy water or biting into a jagged stone buried in a loaf. Being thus interwoven, it does not seem possible that it should escape intact, extricating itself undamaged from every sinew, bone and joint. Or, if you suppose that, after being slipped in from outside, the spirit oozes through our limbs, then it is all the more bound to perish with the body through which it is thus interfused.

To ooze through something is to be dissolved in it and therefore to perish. We know that food, when it is apportioned out amongst our limbs and members by diffusion through all the channels of the body, is destroyed, taking on a different nature. Likewise, on the assumption that spirit and mind enter into the newly formed body as complete entities, they must be dissolved in oozing through it: our limbs must be interpenetrated through every channel by the particles composing this mind which lords it now in our body.

This new mind born of the old one that must have perished in its diffusion through our limbs, becoming evident that the human spirit is neither deprived of a birthday nor immune from a funeral.

A new question arises whether or not any atoms of vital spirit are left in a lifeless body.

If some are left and lodge there, we are not justified in regarding the spirit as immortal, since it has come away mutilated by the loss of some of its parts. If, on the other hand, it leaves with its members intact, so that no scrap of it remains in the body, how is it that corpses, when their flesh begins to rot, beget maggots? What is the source of that boneless and bloodless horde of animate things that swarms through the swollen limbs? You may argue that spirits can slip into the maggots from outside and settle individually in their bodies. I will not ask why in that case many thousands of spirits should assemble in the place from which one has withdrawn.

But there is another question that calls for a decisive answer.

Do these supposed spirits each hunt out atoms of maggots and manufacture dwelling-places for themselves? Or do they slip into ready-made bodies? No adequate reason can be given why they should undertake the labor of manufacture. In their bodiless state they presumably flit about untroubled by sickness, cold or hunger. The body is far more susceptible to these afflictions, and communion with it is the source of many of the mind's troubles. But suppose they had the best of reasons for making a body to which they could subject themselves: there is no discernible way in which they could set about it.

So much for the belief that spirits make bodies and limbs for themselves!

We may equally rule out the alternative theory that they slip into ready-made bodies. For this would not account for the intimate communion between body and spirit and their sensory interaction. Again, why is ferocity an attribute of the lions' surly breed, as craftiness of foxes? Why are deer endowed by their fathers with timidity and their limbs impelled to flight by hereditary panic? Why are all other traits of this sort implanted in physique and character from birth? It can only be because the mind always shares in the specific growth of the body according to its seed and breed.

If the spirit were immortal and passed from body to body, there would be living creatures of confused characters. Often the hound of Hyrcanian breed would turn tail before the onset of the antlered stag. The hawk would flee trembling through the gusty air at the coming of the dove. Man would be witless and brute beasts rational.

It is an untenable theory that an immortal spirit is modified by a change of body.

We see that whatever body changes is disintegrated and therefore destroyed. The component parts of spirits are in any case transposed and reshuffled. So the spirits as a whole might just as well be diffused through the limbs and eventually destroyed with the body. However, If it is held that the spirits of men enter none but human bodies, then I would ask why a wise one should become foolish — why a child is never sensible, nor a mare's foal as accomplished as a sturdy steed.

The one loophole left is the assumption that in a frail body the mind too grows frail. But in that case you must admit that the spirit is mortal, since in its adaptation to the bodily frame it loses so utterly its previous vitality and sensibility. How can the mind wax strong in unison with each particular body till it attains with it the coveted season of full bloom, unless the two are co-heirs of a single birth? Why, when the limbs are fraught with age, should the mind wish to slip out and away? Is it afraid to stay locked up in a moldering body? Afraid that its lodging may collapse from the wear and tear of age? Surely an immortal being need fear *no* danger.

It surely seems ridiculous to suppose that spirits are

standing by at the mating and birth of animals: countless immortals on the look-out for mortal frames, jostling and squabbling to get in first and establish themselves most firmly. Or is there perhaps an established contract that first come shall be first served, without any trial of strength between spirit and spirit?

[Soul and mind like all other things, have their appointed place, apart from which they cannot exists] A tree cannot exist high in air, or clouds in the depths of the sea, as fish cannot live in the fields, or blood flow in wood or sap in stones. There is a determined and allotted place for the growth and place of everything. Likewise, mind cannot arise alone without body or apart from sinews and blood. If it could do this, then surely it could much more readily function in head or shoulders or the tips of the heels and be born in any other part, provided it was held in the same container, that is to say in the same man.

But even in the human body we see a fixed and allotted place set aside for the growth and presence of spirit and mind, we have even stronger reasons for denying that they could survive or come to birth outside the body altogether.

[The union of mortal and immortal is absurd] You must admit, therefore, that when the body has perished there is an end also of the spirit ripped to shreds throughout the body. It is surely insane to couple a mortal object with an eternal and suppose that they can work in harmony and mutually interact.

What can be thought more incongruous, more repugnant and discordant, than that a mortal object and one that is immortal and everlasting should unite to form a compound and jointly weather the storms that rage about them?

So, there can be only three kinds of everlasting objects:

The *first,* one of absolute solidity of substance that can repel blows, letting nothing penetrate them so as to unknit their close texture from within. Such are the atoms of matter, whose nature I have already demonstrated. The *second* kind can last forever given it is immune from blows. Such is empty space, which remains untouched and unscathed by any impact. *Third* is that which has no available place surrounding it into which its matter can disperse and disintegrate. It is for this reason that the grand total of the universe is everlasting, having no space outside it into which the matter can escape and no matter that can enter and disintegrate it by the force of impact.

Equally foolish is the suggestion that the spirit is immortal because it is shielded by life-preserving powers: or because it is spared by forces hostile to its survival; or because such forces, if they threaten, are somehow repelled before we are conscious of the threat. Common sense makes it obvious that this cannot be the case apart from the spirit's participation in the ailments of the body, it has maladies enough of its own. The prospect of the future torments it with fear and wearies it with worry, the past misdeeds leaving the sting of remorse.

Lastly, it may fall a prey to the mind's own specific afflictions, madness and amnesia, plunging into the black waters of oblivion.

[Death is nothing to us. We shall not be conscious after death] From all this we conclude that *death is nothing to us* and no concern of ours, since the nature of the mind is now held to be mortal.

In the olden days we felt no disquiet when the hosts of Carthage poured in to battle on every side — when the whole earth, dizzied by the convulsive shock of war, reeled sickeningly under the high ethereal vault and between realm and realm the empire of mankind by land and sea trembled in the balance. So, when we shall be no more; when the union of body and spirit that engenders us has been disrupted—we shall then be nothing; nothing since no hazard will happen anymore at all.

Nothing will have power to stir our senses, not though earth be fused with sea and sea with sky.

If any feeling remains in mind or spirit after it has been torn from our body—that is nothing to us, who are brought into being by the wedlock of body and spirit, conjoined and coalesced.

Or even if the matter that composes us should be reassembled by time after our death and brought back into its present state; if the light of life were given to us anew, even that contingency would still be no concern of ours once the chain of our identity had been snapped. We who are *now* are not concerned with ourselves in any previous existence: the sufferings of those selves do not touch us.

Looking at the immeasurable extent of time gone by and the multiform movements of matter, you will readily accept that these same atoms that compose us now must many a time before have entered into the selfsame combinations as now. But our mind cannot recall this to remembrance. For between then and now is interposed a break in life, and all the atomic motions have been wandering far astray from sentience.

If the future holds misery and anguish in store, the self must be in existence, when that time comes, in order to be miserable. But from this fate we are saved by death, which denies existence to the self that might have suffered these tribulations.

Rest assured, therefore, that we have nothing to fear in death.

One who no longer *is* cannot suffer, or differ in any way from one who has never been born, when once this mortal life has been usurped by death the immortal.

[A believer in the mortality of the soul is often insincere] When you find a man treating it as a grievance that after death he will either molder in the grave or fall a prey to flames or to the jaws of predatory beasts, be sure that his complaint does not ring true. Subconsciously his heart is stabbed by a secret dread, however loudly the man himself may disavow the belief that after death he will still experience sensation. I am convinced that he does not grant the admission he professes, or the grounds of it; he does not oust and pluck himself root and branch out of life, but all unwittingly makes something of himself linger on.

[He imagines a Self that survives to grieve at the fate of

the body] When a living man faces the thought that after death his body will be mauled by birds and beasts prey, he is filled with self-pity. He does not banish himself from the scene nor distinguish sharply enough between himself and that abandoned carcass. Visualizing that object as himself he infects it with his own feelings as an onlooker. That is why he is aggrieved at having been created mortal. He does not see that in real death there will be *no* other self-alive to mourn his own decease —no other self-standing by to flinch at the agony he suffers lying there being mangled, or indeed being cremated. For if it is really a bad thing after death to be mauled and crunched by ravening jaws, I cannot see why it should not be disagreeable to roast in the scorching flames of a funeral pyre, or to lie embalmed in honey, stifled and stiff with cold, on the surface of a chilly slab, or to be squashed under a crushing weight of earth.

[**The dead has no more desire for the joys of life**] Now it is all over. Now, neither the happy home and the best of wives will welcome you, nor delightful children rush to snatch the first kiss at your coming, touching your heart with speechless joy. No chance now to further your fortune or safeguard your family. "Unhappy man," they cry, "unhappily cheated by one treacherous day out of all these blessings of life!" But they do not go on to say: "And now no repining for these lost joys will oppress you anymore."

If they saw this clearly with their minds and acted according to the words, they would free their breasts from a great load of grief and dread.

"Ah, yes!" *You* are at peace now in the sleep of death, and so you will stay till the end of time. Pain and sorrow will never touch you again. But to *us,* who stood weeping inconsolably while you were consumed to ashes on the dreadful pyre — to us no day will come that will lift the undying sorrow from our hearts.

Ask the speaker what is so heart-rending about this. If something returns to sleep and peace, what reason is that for pining in inconsolable grief?

Here again, is the way men often talk from the bottom of their hearts when they recline at a banquet, goblet in hand, brows decked with garlands: "How all too short are these good times that come to us poor creatures! Soon they will be past and gone, and there will be no recalling them." You would think the crowning calamity in store for them after death was to be parched and shriveled by a tormenting thirst or oppressed by some other vain desire. But even in sleep, when mind and body alike are at rest, no one misses himself or sighs for life. If such sleep were prolonged to eternity, no longing for ourselves would trouble us. And yet the vital atoms in our limbs cannot be far removed from their sensory motions at a time when a mere jolt out of sleep enables a man to pull himself together.

As far as we are concerned, death must be regarded as having much less existence than sleep; if anything can have less existence than what we perceive to be nothing. For death is followed by a far greater dispersal of the seething mass of matter: once that icy break in life has intervened, there is no more waking.

[Nature justifiably may reproach us for lamenting our death] Suppose that Nature herself were suddenly to find a voice and round upon one of us in these terms:

"What is your complaint, mortal, that you give yourself up to this whining and repining? Why do you weep and wail over death? If the life you have lived till now has been a pleasant thing —if all its blessings have not leaked away like water poured into a cracked pot and run to waste unrelished— why then, you stupid man, do you not retire like a dinner guest who has eaten his fill of life, and take your carefree rest with a quiet mind? Or, if all your gains have been poured profitless away and life has grown distasteful, why do you seek to swell the total? The new can but turn out as badly as the old and perish as unprofitably. Why not rather make an end of life and trouble? Do you expect me to invent some new contrivance for your pleasure? I tell you, there is none. All things are always the same. If your body is not yet withered with age, nor your limbs decrepit and flagging, even so there is nothing new to look forward to — not though you should outlive all living creatures, or even though you should never die at all."

What are we to answer; except that Nature's rebuff is justified and the plea she puts forward is a true one?

[Nature asks the elder to make way for others] But suppose it is some senior citizen who complains, some dismal greybeard who laments over his nearing end far more than he ought. Would she not have every right to protest more vehemently and repulse him in stern tones:

"Away with your tears, old reprobate! Have done with your grumbling! You are withering now after tasting all the joys of life. But because you are always pining for what is not and ungrateful of the things at hand, your life has slipped away unfulfilled and unrewarded. Death has stolen upon you unawares, before you are ready to retire from life's banquet filled and satisfied. Come now, put away all that is untoward to your years and compose your mind to make way for others. You have no choice."

Unquestionably, she would have right on her side; her censure and rebuff would be well merited. The old is always thrust aside to make way for the new, and one thing must be built out of the wreck of others. There is no murky pit of Tartarus awaiting anyone. There is need of matter, so that later generations may arise; when they have lived out their-span, they will all follow you. Bygone generations have taken your road, and those to come will take it no less.

So, one thing will never cease to spring from another. To none is life given in freehold; to all on lease. Look back at the eternity that passed before we were born, and mark how utterly it counts to us as nothing. This is a mirror that Nature holds up to us, in which we may see the time that shall be after we are dead. Is there anything terrifying in the sight, anything depressing, anything that is not more restful than the soundest sleep?

As for all those torments that are said to take place in the depths of Acheron, they are actually present here and now, in our own lives.

[**Tantalus is religion-oppressed**] There is no wretched Tantalus, as the myth relates, transfixed with groundless terror at the huge boulder poised above him in the air. But in this life there really are mortals tortured by unfounded fear of the gods and trembling at the impending doom that may fall upon any of them at the whim of chance.

There is no Tityos[18] lying in Acheron forever opened up by birds of prey. Assuredly they cannot find food by groping under those giant ribs to glut them throughout eternity. No matter to what length that titanic frame may lie outstretched, so that he covers not a paltry nine acres with his spread-eagled limbs but the whole extent of earth, he will not be able to suffer an eternity of pain nor furnish food from his body for evermore. But Tityos is here in our midst: that poor devil victimized by love, torn indeed by birds of prey, devoured by gnawing anxiety or rent by the fangs of some other passion.

[**Sisyphus the failed public man**] Sisyphus[19] too is alive for all to see, bent on winning the emblem of office, its rods and ruthless axes, by the people's vote, and is embittered by perpetual defeat. To strive for this profitless and never-granted prize, and in striving toil and moil incessantly: to push a boulder laboriously up a steep hill, only to see it, once the top is reached, rolling and bounding down again to the flat levels of the plain.

By the same token, to be forever feeding a malcontent mind, filling it with good things but never satisfying it: the fate we suffer when the circling seasons enrich us with their products and their ever-changing charms although we are never filled with the fruits of life; this of course exemplifies the story of those maidens in the flower of life forever pouring water into a leaking vessel that can never by any technique be filled.

As for Cerberus and the Furies and the pitchy darkness and Tartarus belching abominable fumes from its throat, these do not and cannot exist anywhere at all.

But life is darkened by the fear of retribution for our misdeeds, a fear enormous in proportion to their enormity, and by the penalties imposed for crime — imprisonment and ghastly precipitation from Tarpeia's Rock,[20] the whip, the executioners, the condemned cell, the boiling pitch, the hot metal plates and the flaming torches. Even though these horrors are not physically present, yet the conscience-ridden mind in terrified anticipation torments itself with its own goads and whips. It does not see what term there can be to its suffering or where its punishment can have an end.

[Hell is the fear of punishment in this life] Being frightened that death may serve only to intensify all this pain, at length the lives of misguided mortals become a Hell on earth.

Here is something that you might well say to yourself from time to time:

"Even good king Ancus contemplated his last on the daylight, a better man than you, my presumptuous friend, by a long way. Death has come to many another monarch and potentate, who ruled over mighty nations. Even that King of Kings[21] who once built a highway across the great deep sea, who gave his legions a path to tread among the waves and taught them to march on foot over the briny gulfs and with his chargers trampled scornfully upon the ocean's roar — even he was robbed of the light and poured out the spirit from a dying frame. Scipio, that thunderbolt of war, the terror of Carthage, gave his bones to the earth as if he had been the meanest of serfs. Add to this company the discoverers of truth and beauty. Add the attendants of the Muses, among them Homer, who in solitary glory bore the scepter but has sunk into the same slumber as the rest. Democritus, when ripe age warned him that the mindful motions of his intellect were running down, made his unbowed head a willing sacrifice to death. And the master himself, when his day-time race was run, Epicurus himself died, whose genius outshone the race of men and dimmed them all, as the stars are dimmed by the rising of the fiery sun.

And will *you* kick and protest against your sentence?

[Life is a waking sleep] You, whose life is next-door to death although you still live and look on the light. You, who waste the major part of your time in sleep and, when you are awake, are snoring still and dreaming. You, who bear a mind hag-ridden by groundless fear and cannot find the commonest cause of your distress, hounded as you are, pathetic creature, by a pack of troubles and drifting in a drunken stupor upon a wavering tide of fantasy.

[Men live restless lives due to uncertainty] Men feel plainly enough within their minds a heavy burden, whose weight depresses them. If only they perceived with equal clearness the causes of this depression, the origin of this lump of evil within their breasts, they would not lead such a life as we now see all too commonly: no one knowing what he really wants, and everyone forever trying to get away from where he is, as though travel alone could throw off the load.

The owner of some stately mansion, bored stiff by staying at home, we often see takes his departure, only to return as speedily when he feels himself no better off put of doors. Off he goes to his country seat, driving his Gaulish ponies hotfoot, as though rushing to save a house on fire. No sooner has he crossed its doorstep than he starts yawning or retires moodily to sleep and courts oblivion, or else rushes back to revisit the city. In so doing the individual is really running away from himself. Since he remains reluctantly wedded to the self whom he cannot of course escape, he grows to hate him, because he is a sick man ignorant of the cause of his malady. If he did but see this, he would cast other thoughts aside and devote himself first to studying the nature of the universe. It is not the fortune of an hour that is in question, but of all time; the lot in store for mortals throughout the eternity that awaits them after death.

[A longer life will give no new pleasure] What is this deplorable lust for life that holds us trembling in bondage to such uncertainties and dangers? A fixed term is given to the life of mortals, and there is no way of dodging death. In any case the setting of our lives remains the same throughout, and by going on living we do not mint any new coin of pleasure. So long as the object of our craving is unattained, it seems more precious than anything besides. Once it is ours, we crave for something else. So an unquenchable thirst for life keeps us always on the gasp.

[Prolonging life doesn't diminish the period of death]
There is no foretelling what fortune the future may bring; what chance may throw in our way, or what upshot lies in waiting. By prolonging life, we cannot subtract or whittle away one jot from the duration of our death. The time after our taking off remains constant. However many generations you may add to your store by living, there waits for you none the less the same eternal death.

The period of not-being will be no less for him who made an end of life with today's daylight than for him who perished many a moon and many a year ago.

NOTES

[1] Greek god of the west wind.
[2] Memmius, a distinguished Roman: Gaius Memmius, married to a daughter of the dictator Sulla. Although a political enemy of Julius Cesar, he was appointed to several important posts, falling into disgrace for which he was exiled.
[3] Meaning Epicurus the Greek philosopher.
[4] At Aulis (in Boeotia) King Agamemnon, to placate Artemis (the virgin goddess) and cause the wind to blow the fleet to Troy (to fight the Trojan War) sacrifices his daughter Iphigenia.
[5] Roman poet (239-169 BC), A believer in reincarnation, claims at the beginning of his *Annales* that his soul had been Homer first and later Pythagoras in earlier existences.
[6] Lucretius is alluding to Poseidon, Polyphemus, and the immortality of the Greek gods.
[7] Helen of Troy
[8] Lucretius is referring to the Empedocles' four elements.
[9] Heraclitus, the somber philosopher spoke in riddles, often using impenetrable antitheses. He believed that the universe was a continuous flux: ." ... changes and nothing remains still ... and ... *you cannot step twice*

into the same stream"
[10] Anaximenes of Miletus
[11] Thales of Miletus
[12] Anaxagoras of Clazomenae, Asia Minor (500 – 428 BC), lived in Athens most of his life, where he befriended Pericles and Euripides. By claiming that the sun wasn't a divinity but a red-hot stone, he was charged with impiety and exiled.
[13] It is astonishing to see that in this passage Lucretius is anticipating that atoms have a nucleus and those electrons, positrons, and other atomic constituents might the cause of motion. In this respect, he was way ahead of the theories designed by Aristotle.
[14] Lucretius alludes to the sexual act, which he will treat in depth in Book IV, Sensation and Sex.
[15] Lucretius means the Phrygian Cybele, the Great Mother, goddess of fecundity ironically served by castrated priests called Corybantes
[16] Meaning the Stoic philosophers.
[17] Lucretius is addressing Epicurus
[18] A giant whose liver is eaten by vultures, in punishment for attempting to rape Leto.
[19] Condemned to roll a boulder uphill to an unreachable top.
[20] From the Tarpeian Rock, criminals sentenced to death were flung.
[21] Meaning: Xerxes King of Persia who crossed the Hellespont by building pontoon bridges.

CPSIA information can be obtained
at www.ICGtesting.com
Printed in the USA
LVHW050142240122
709154LV00019B/3252